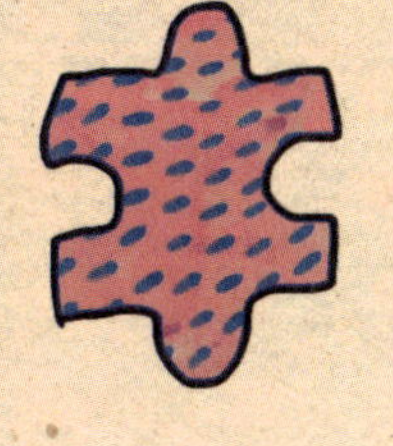



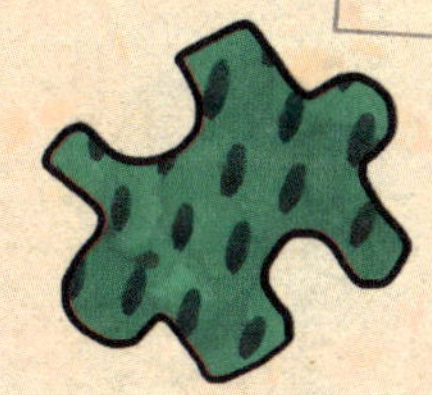

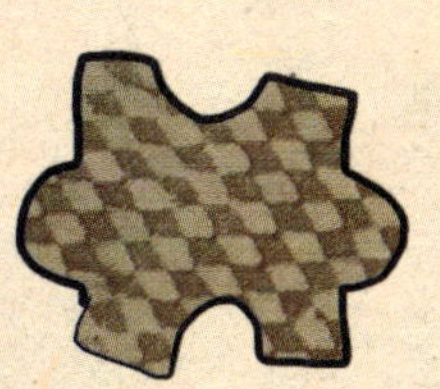

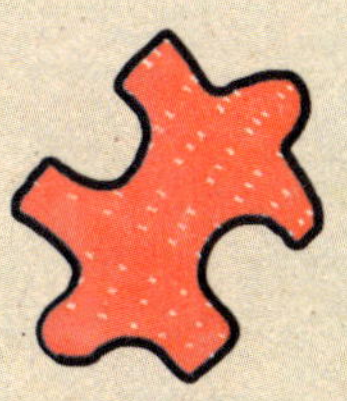

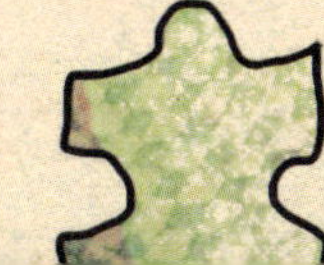

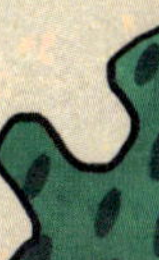

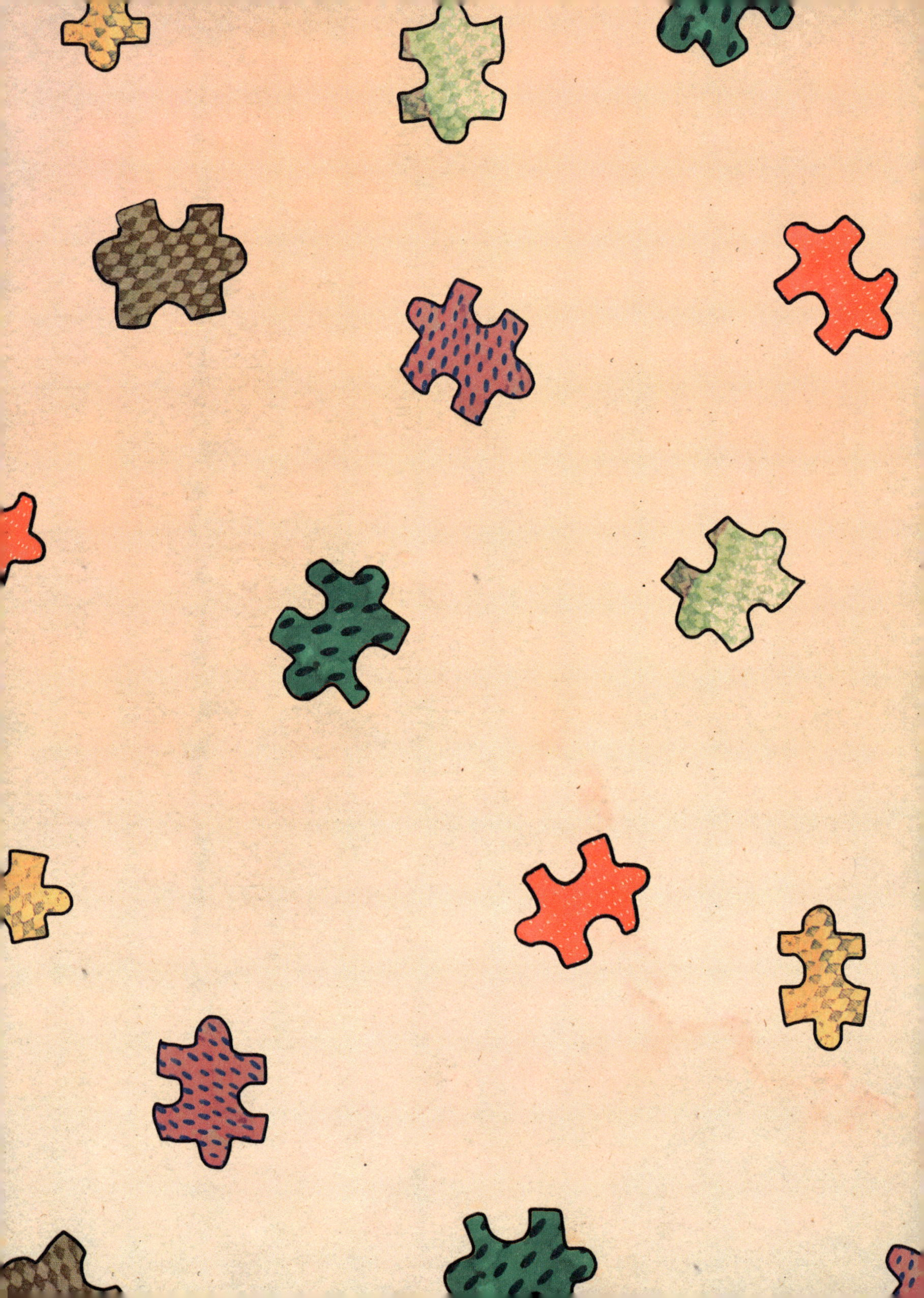

# BETWEEN TWO WORLDS

## THE ART AND LIFE OF AMRITA SHER-GIL

story by Meera Sriram
illustrated by Ruchi Bakshi Sharma

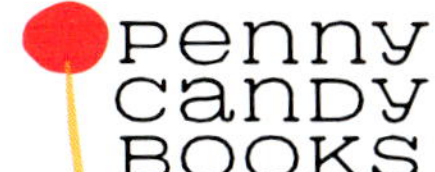

Penny Candy Books
Oklahoma City & Greensboro

This book is printed on paper certified to the environmental and social standards of the Forest Stewardship Council™ (FSC®).

Photo of Meera Sriram: Sriram Gopalakrishnan
Photo of Ruchi Bakshi Sharma: Nehmat Mongia
Design: Shanna Compton Photo of and paintings by Sher-Gil: public domain

Small press. Big conversations.
www.pennycandybooks.com

Library of Congress Cataloging-in-Publication Data

Names: Sriram, Meera, author. | Sharma, Ruchi Bakshi, illustrator.
Title: Between two worlds : the art and life of Amrita Sher-Gil / story by Meera Sriram ; illustrated by Ruchi Bakshi Sharma.
Description: Oklahoma City : Penny Candy Books, 2021. | Includes bibliographical references. | Audience: Ages 7-11 | Audience: Grades 2-3
Identifiers: LCCN 2021016616 (print) | LCCN 2021016617 (ebook) | ISBN 9781734225945 (hardcover) | ISBN 9781736031964 (epub) | ISBN 9781736031964 (mobi) | ISBN 9781736031964 (pdf)
Subjects: LCSH: Sher-Gil, Amrita, 1913-1941--Juvenile literature. | Painters--India--Biography--Juvenile literature.
Classification: LCC ND1010.S5 S69 2021 (print) | LCC ND1010.S5 (ebook) | DDC 759.954--dc2
LC record available at
LC ebook record avai )16617
25 24 23 22 21 1 2 3 4 5

To Rasika and Pritam:
May you continue to grow into global citizens.

—MS

For Jadoo and Mayagauri—
brother sunshine and sister moon,
two magical beings who light up my world.

—RBS

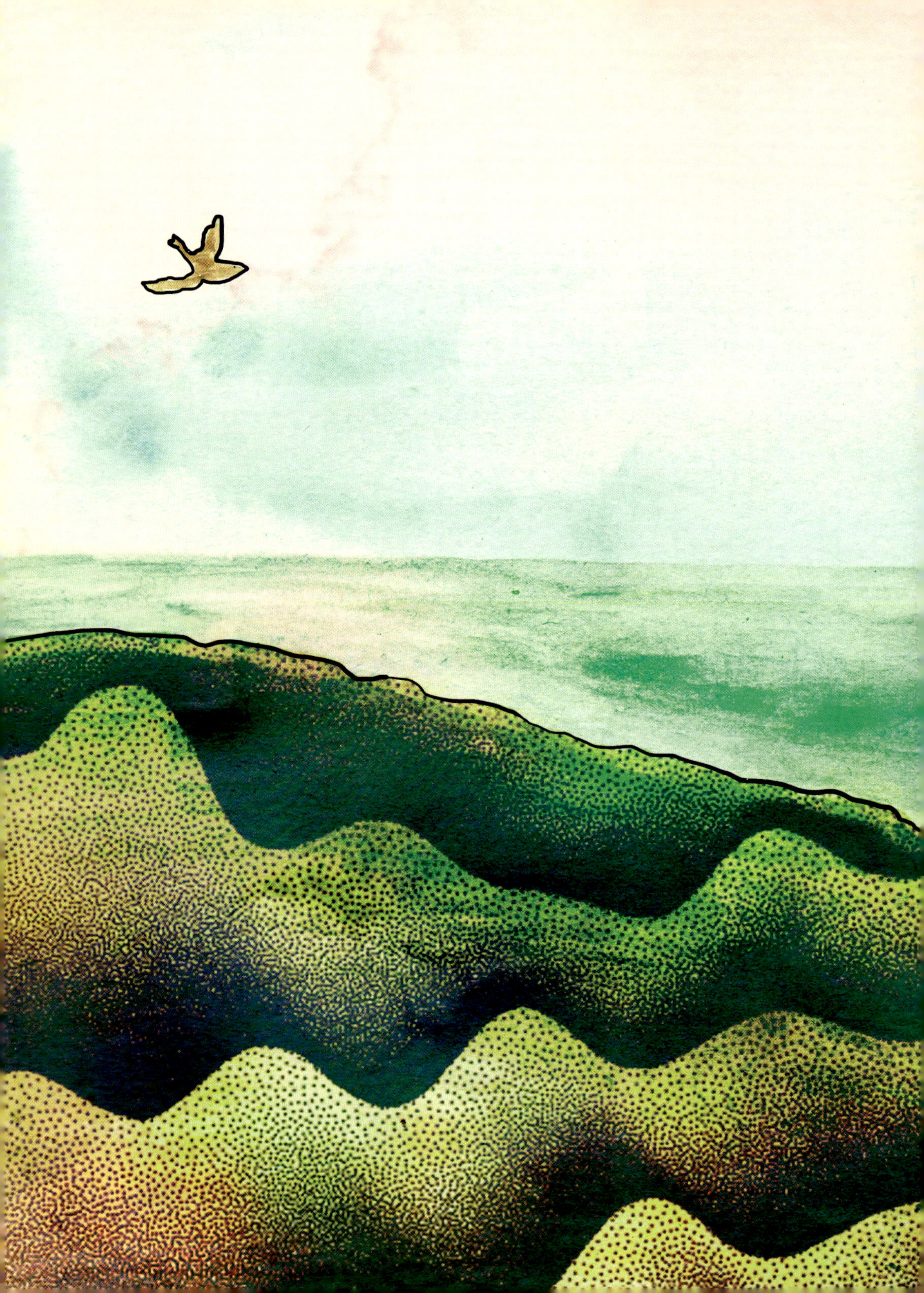

In a quiet village in Hungary, along waters and inside playrooms, little Amrita poured out her imagination—

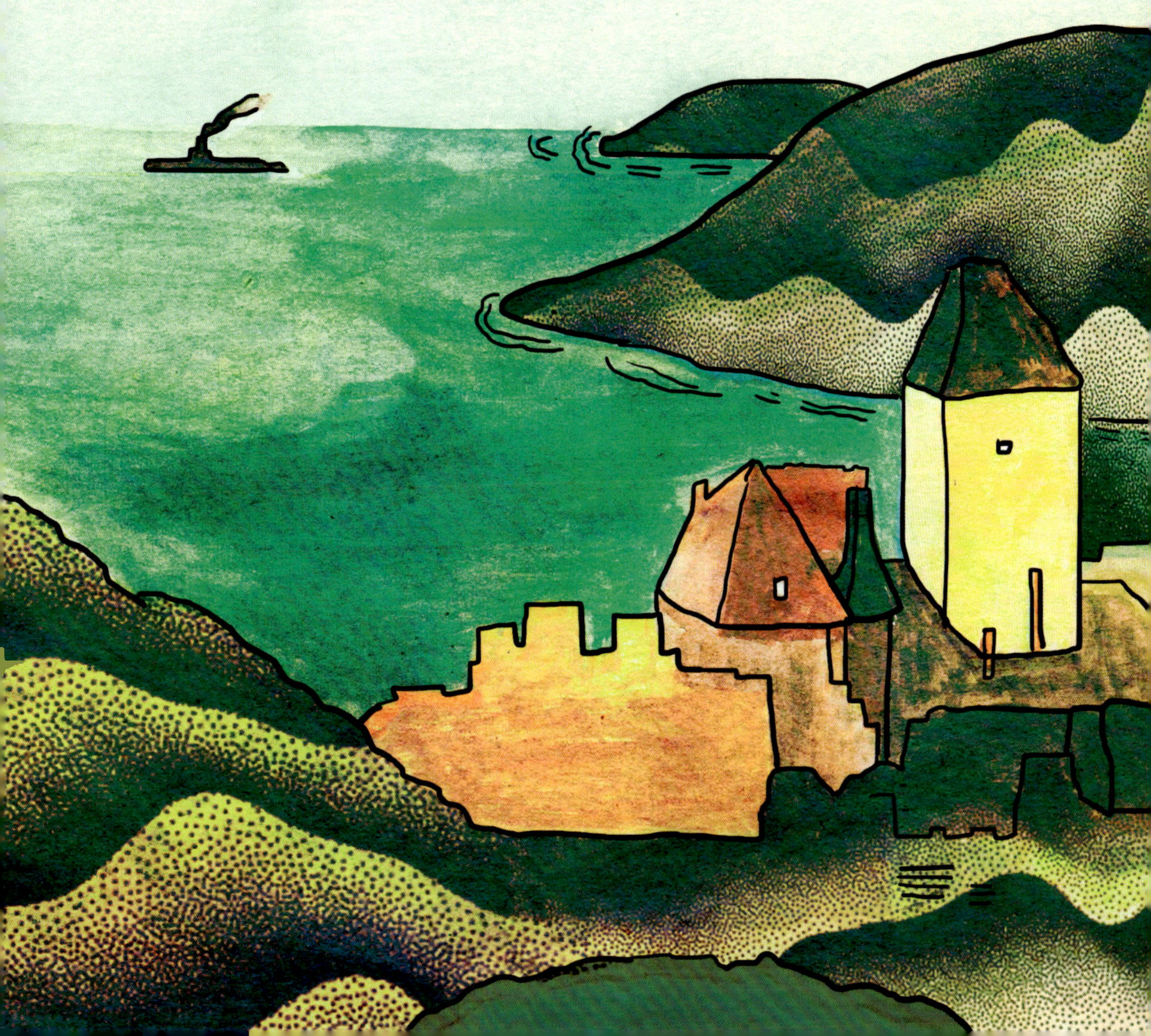

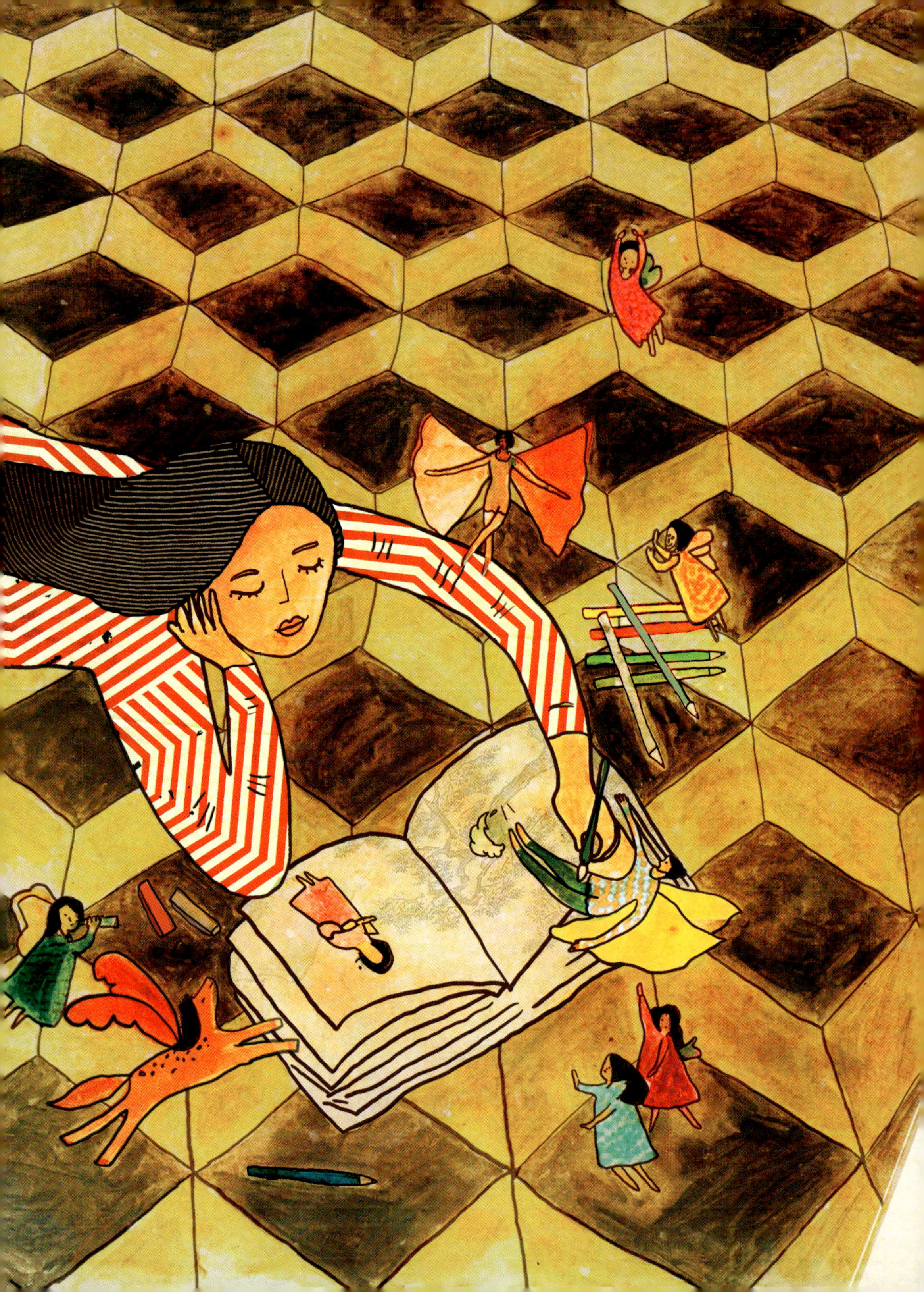

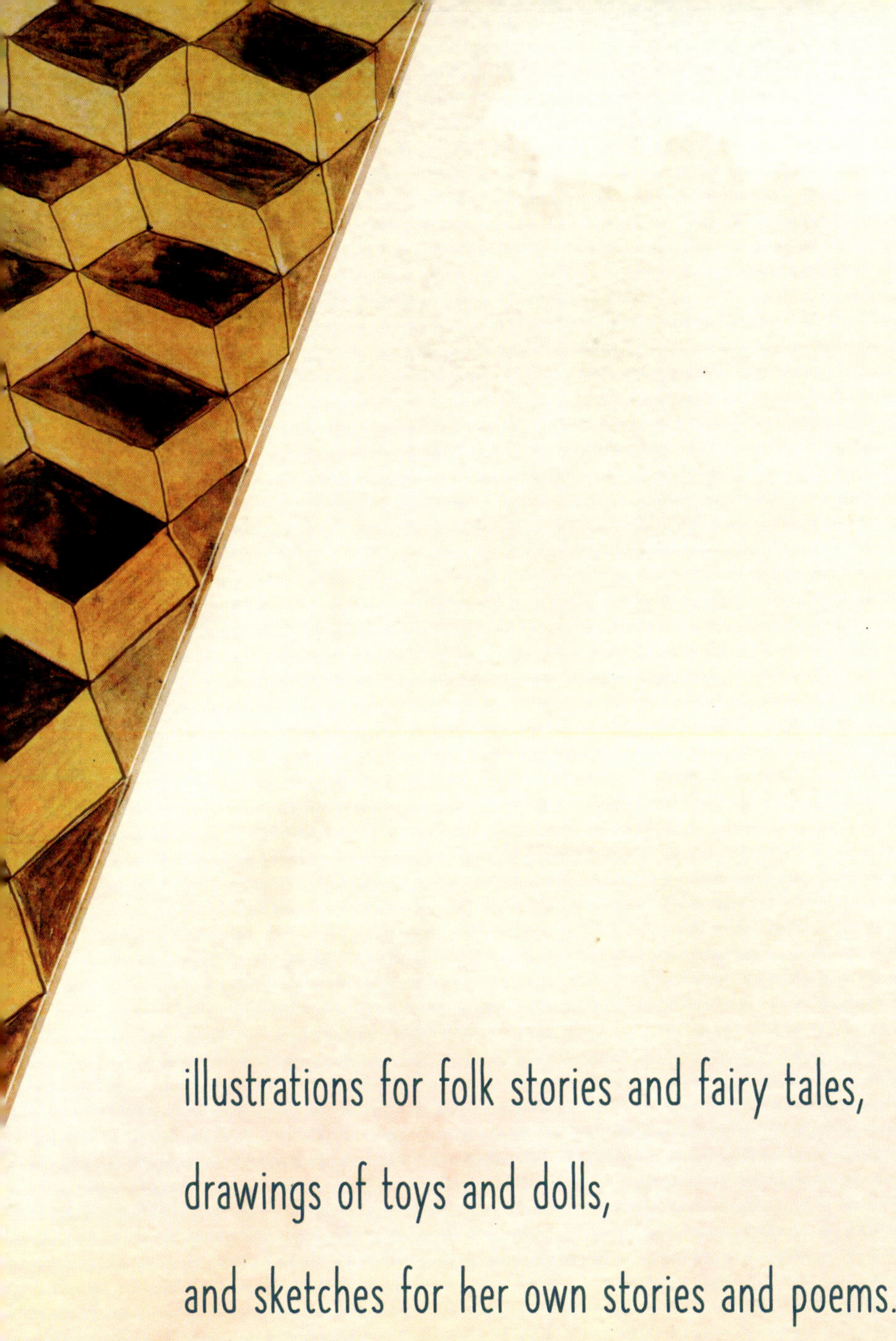

illustrations for folk stories and fairy tales,

drawings of toys and dolls,

and sketches for her own stories and poems.

When she wasn't drawing, she played with her cousins and wandered in gardens.

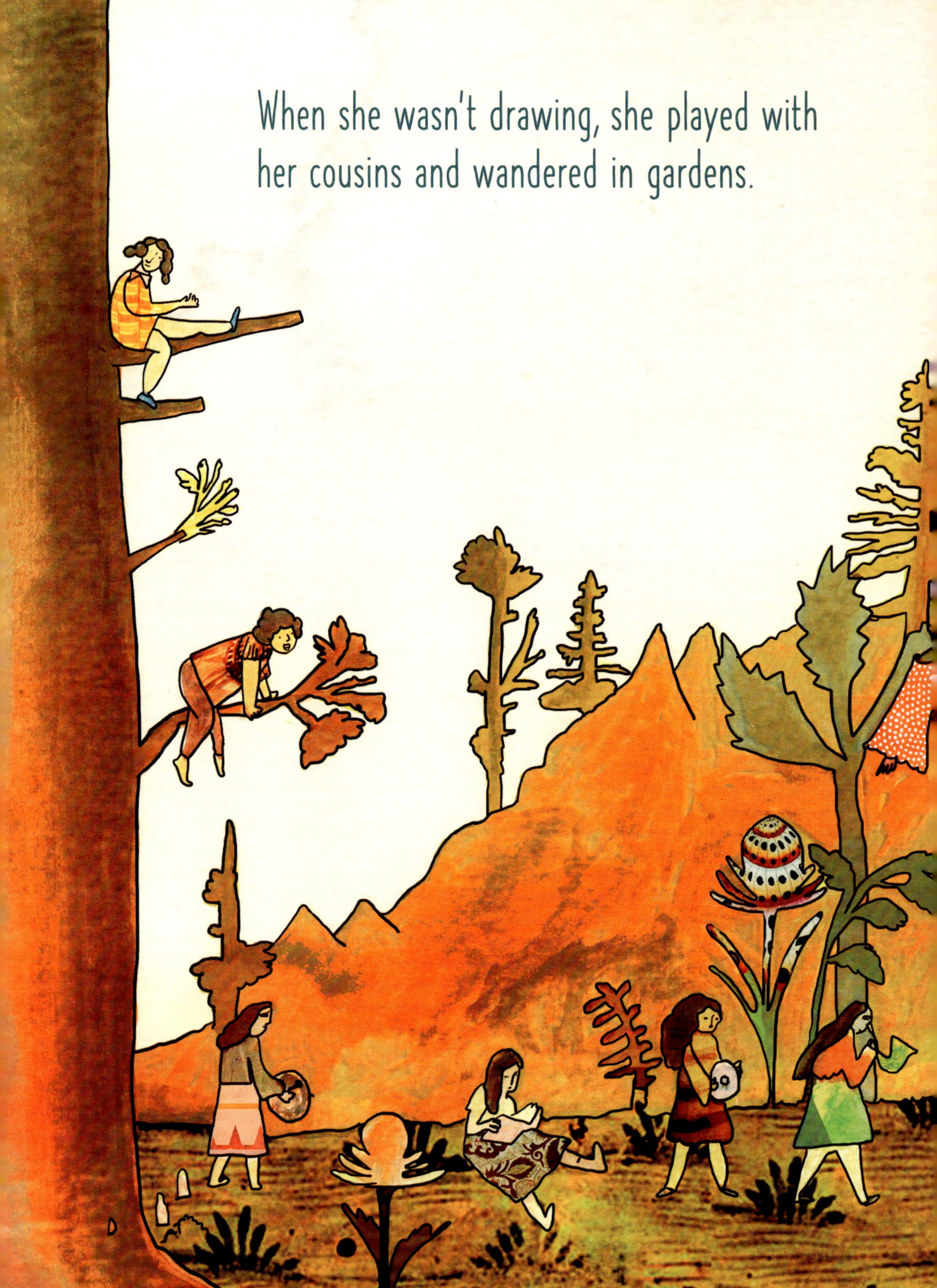

But her world would soon change.

Amrita would begin a lifelong search to find home, to find her own art.

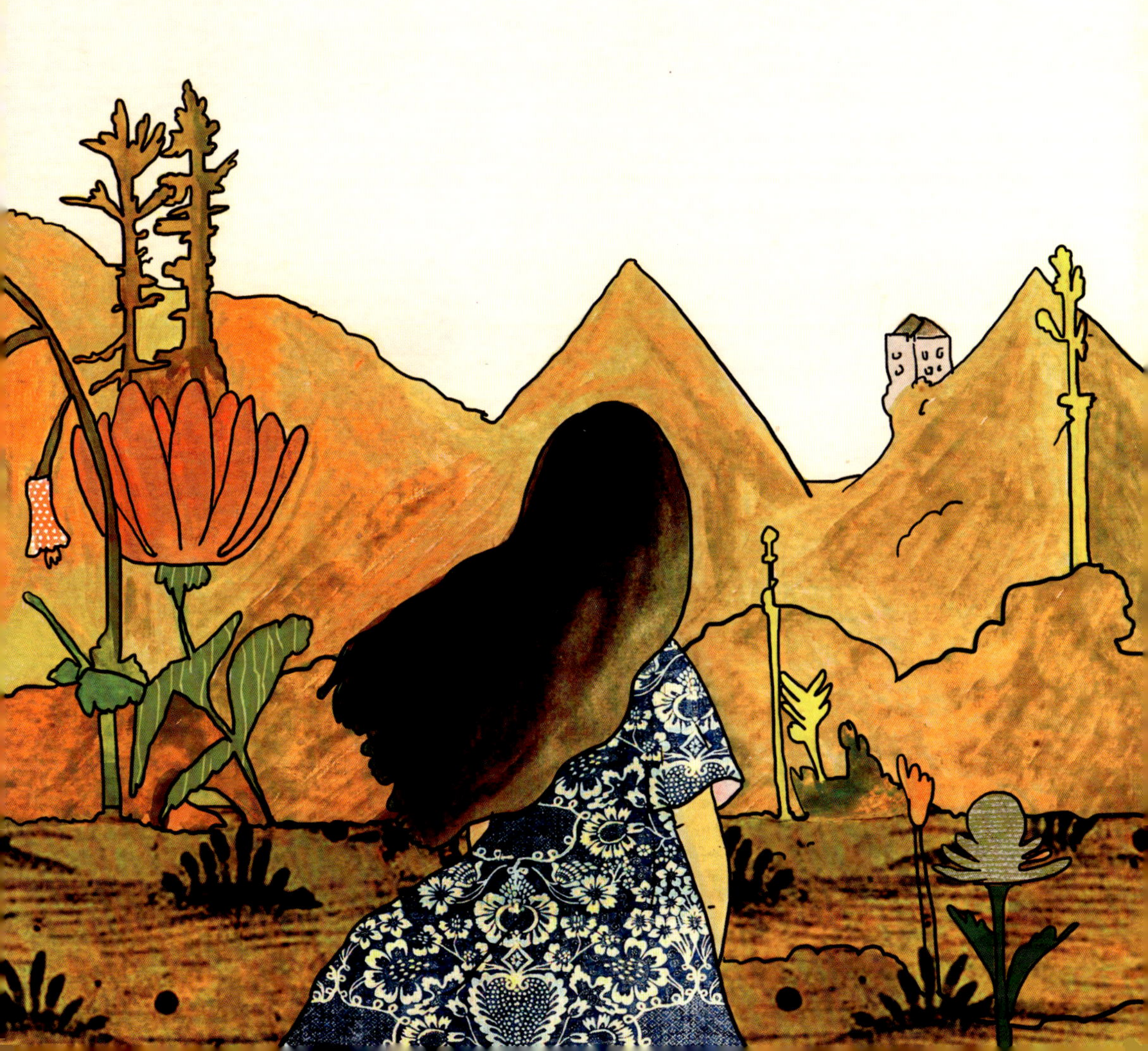

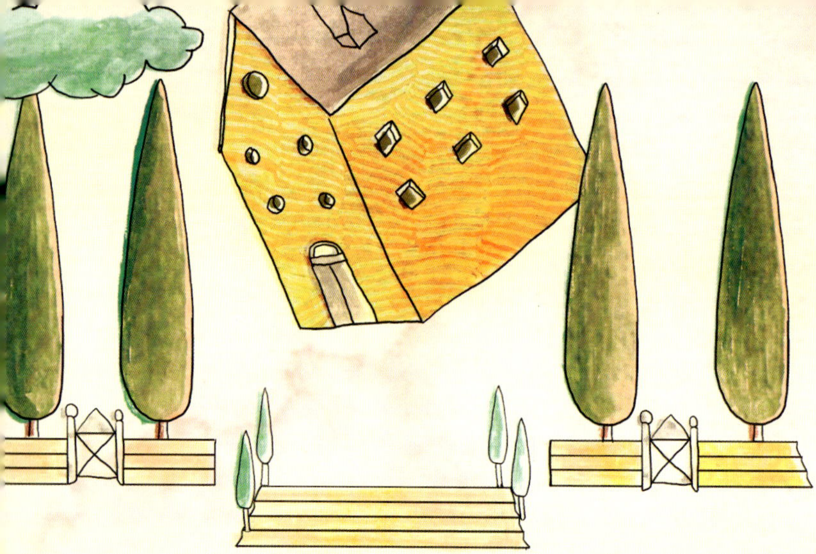

One wintry morning, Amrita and her family said goodbye to Hungary, her mother's country. It was time for them to go to India, her father's home.

Amrita was only eight.

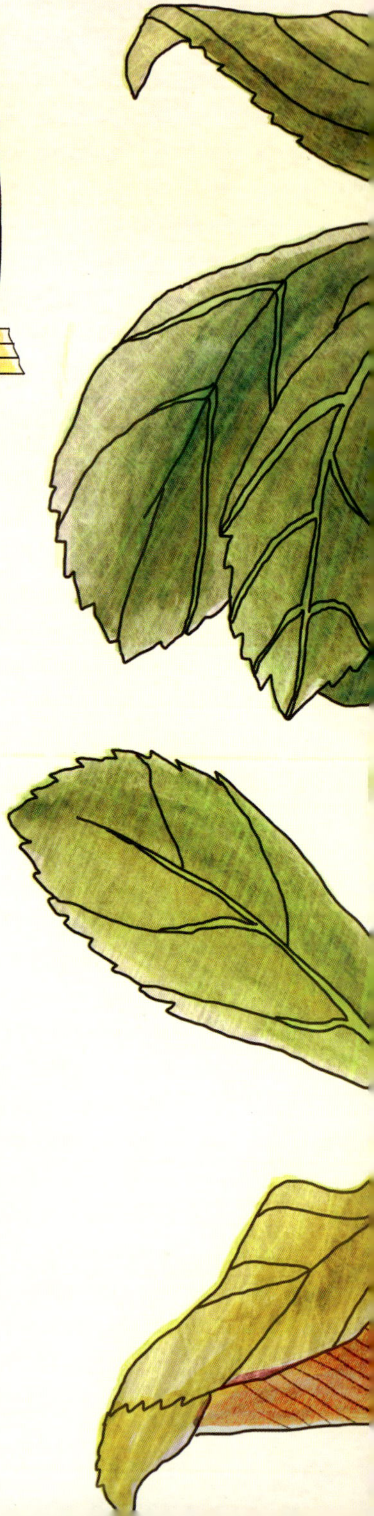

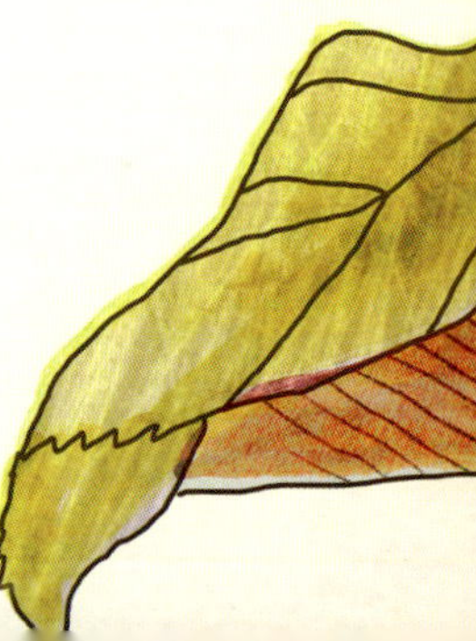

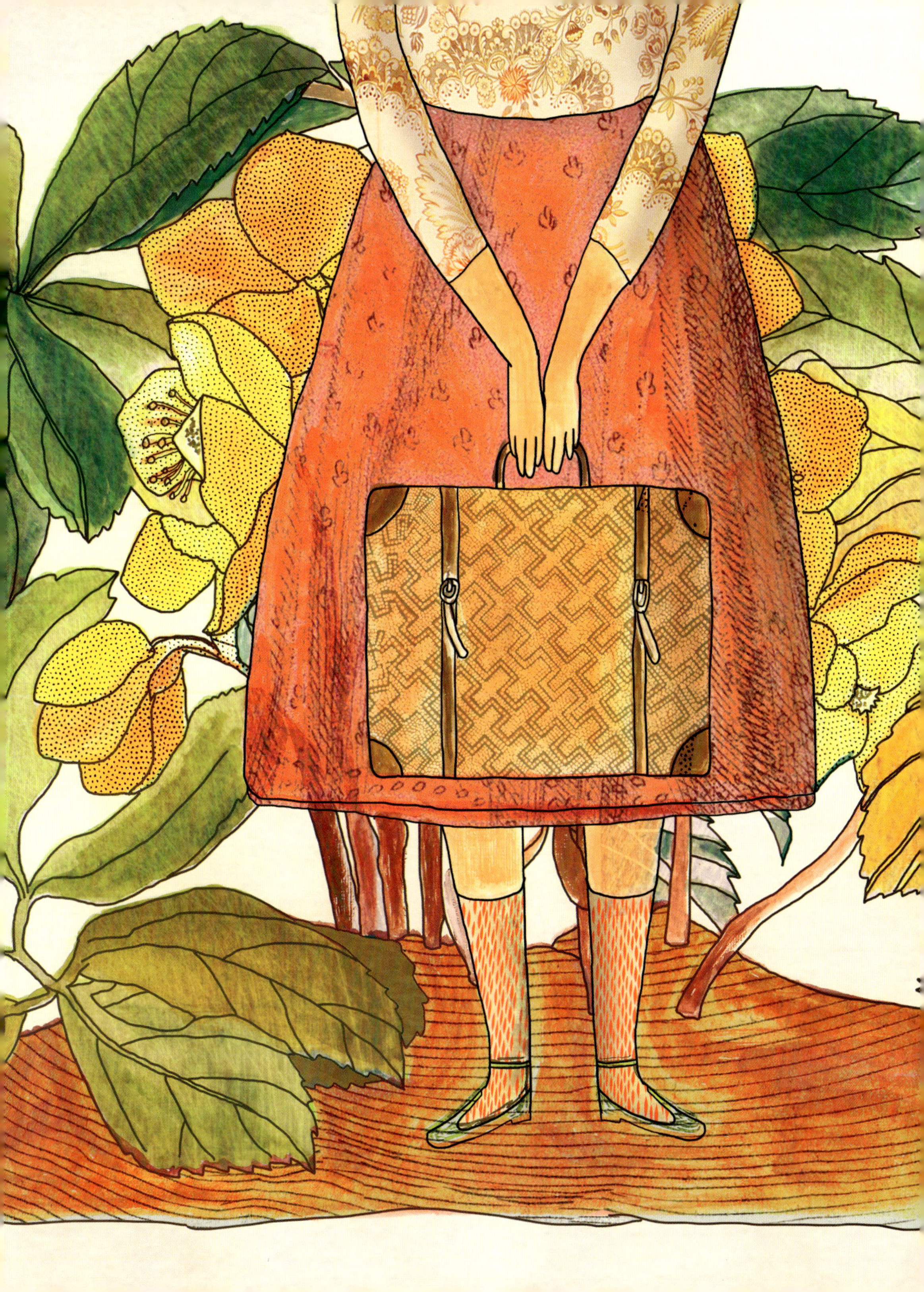

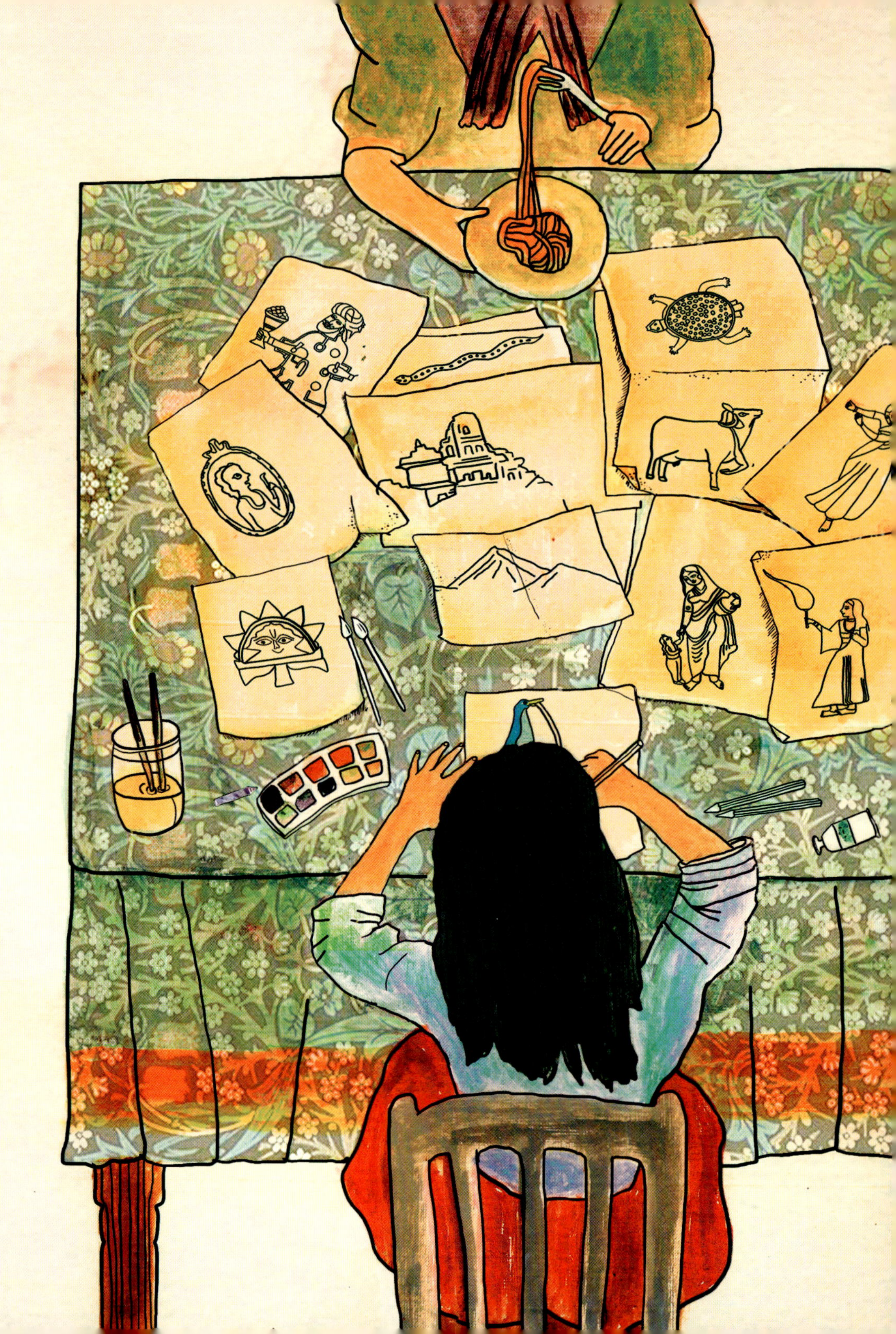

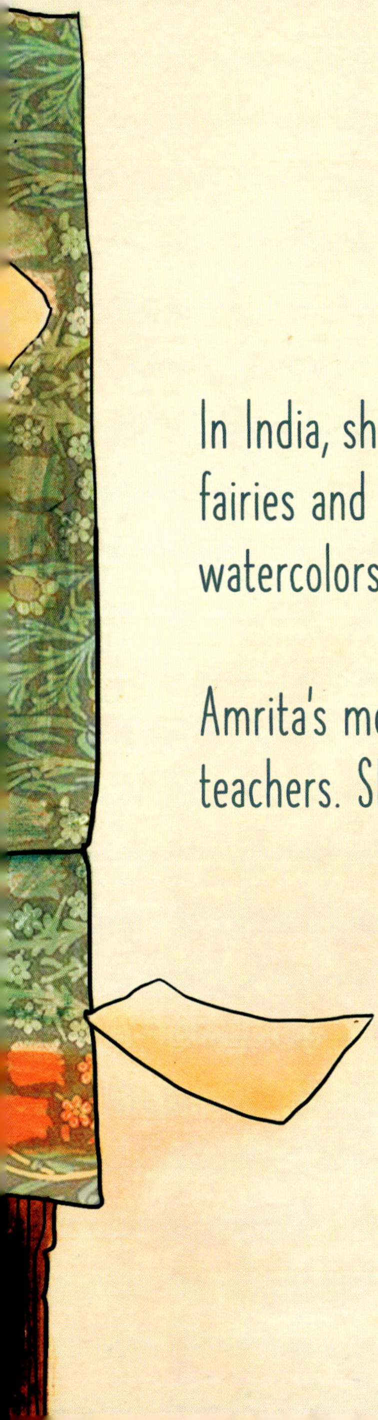

In India, she filled a fresh notebook with fairies and little girls blotched in beautiful watercolors.

Amrita's mother noticed her talent and hired teachers. She took her to an art school.

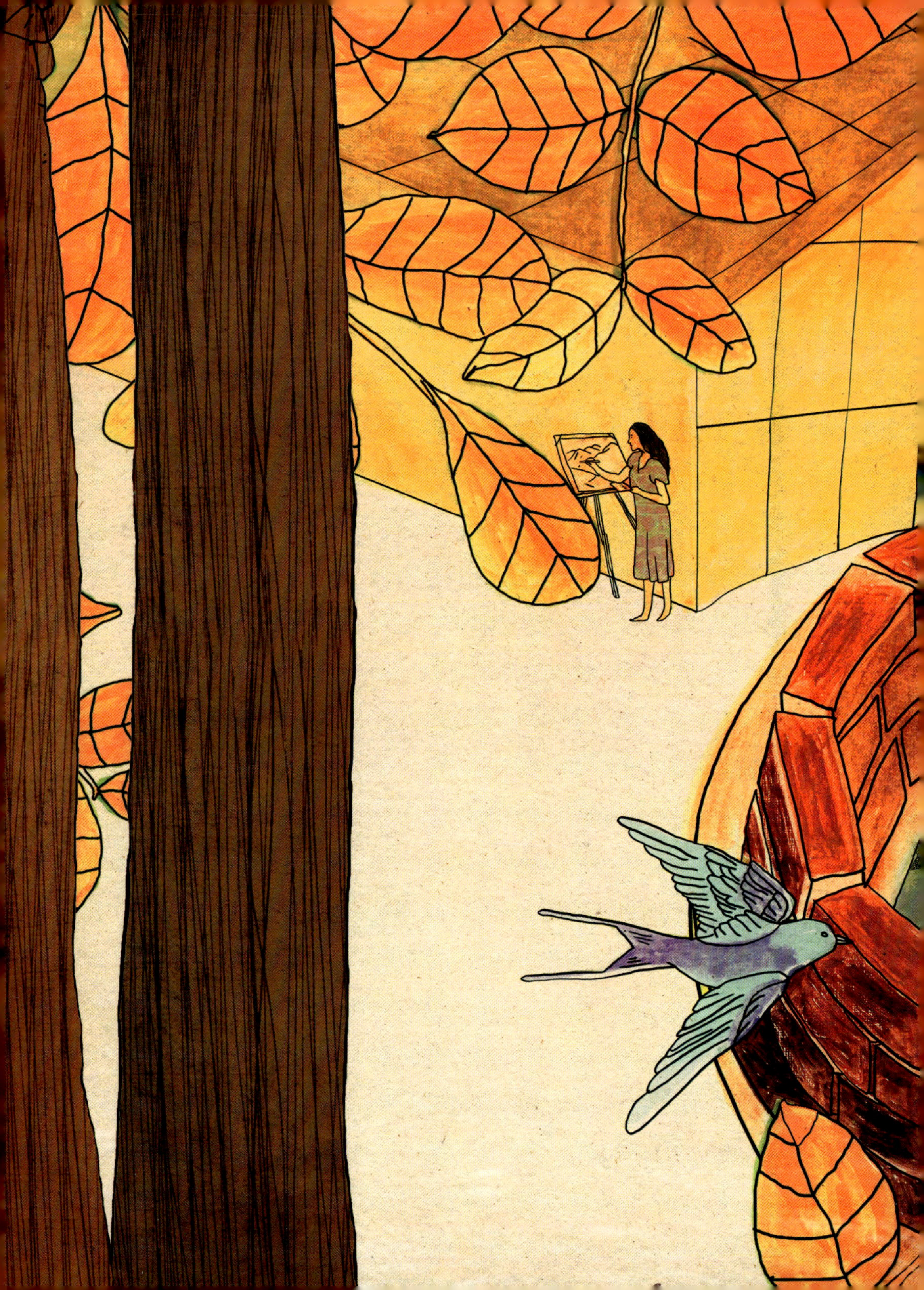

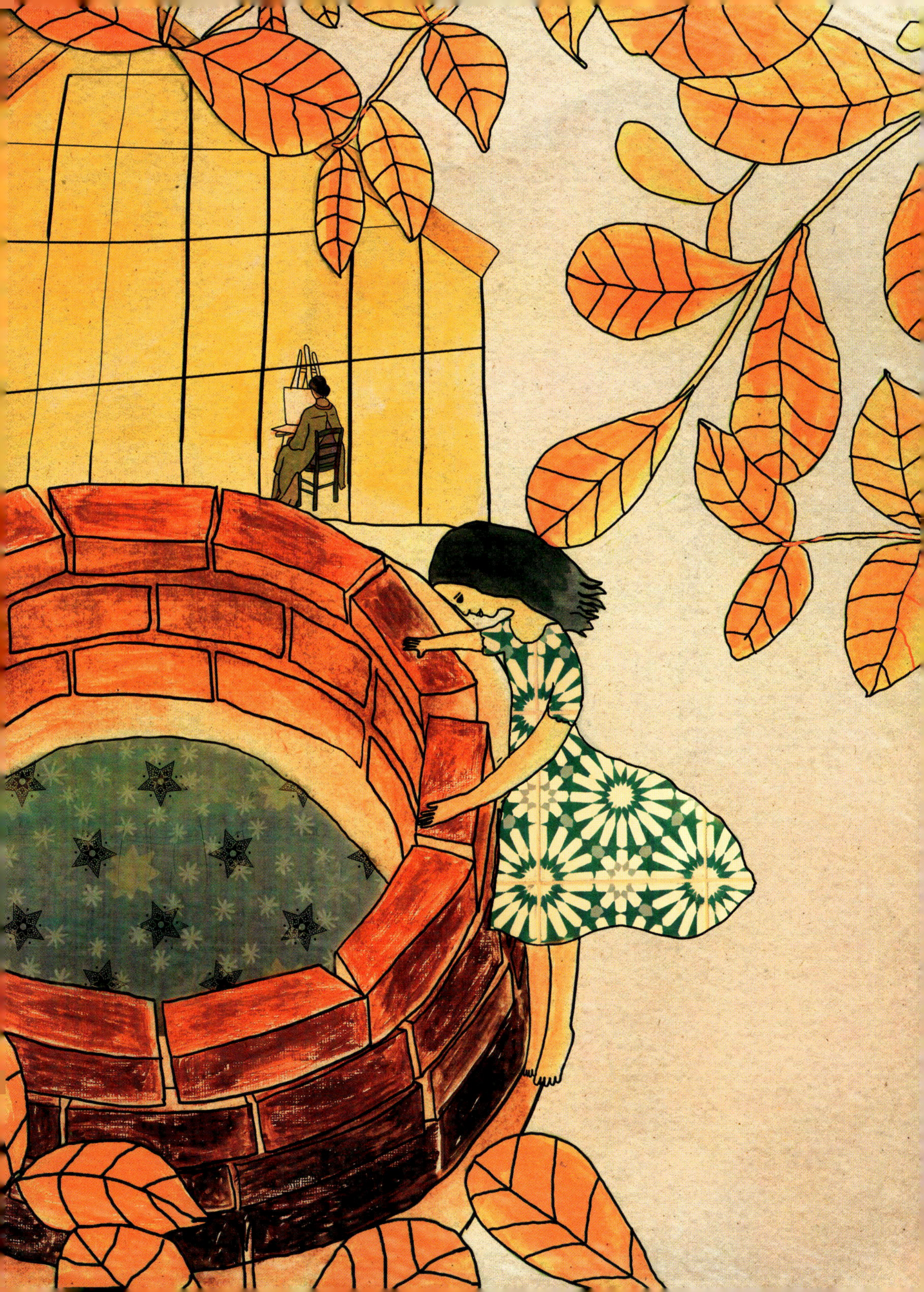

However, art lessons bored Amrita;
she believed art came from the heart.

She rebelled.

She drew on her own terms.

She searched in her art for where
she belonged.

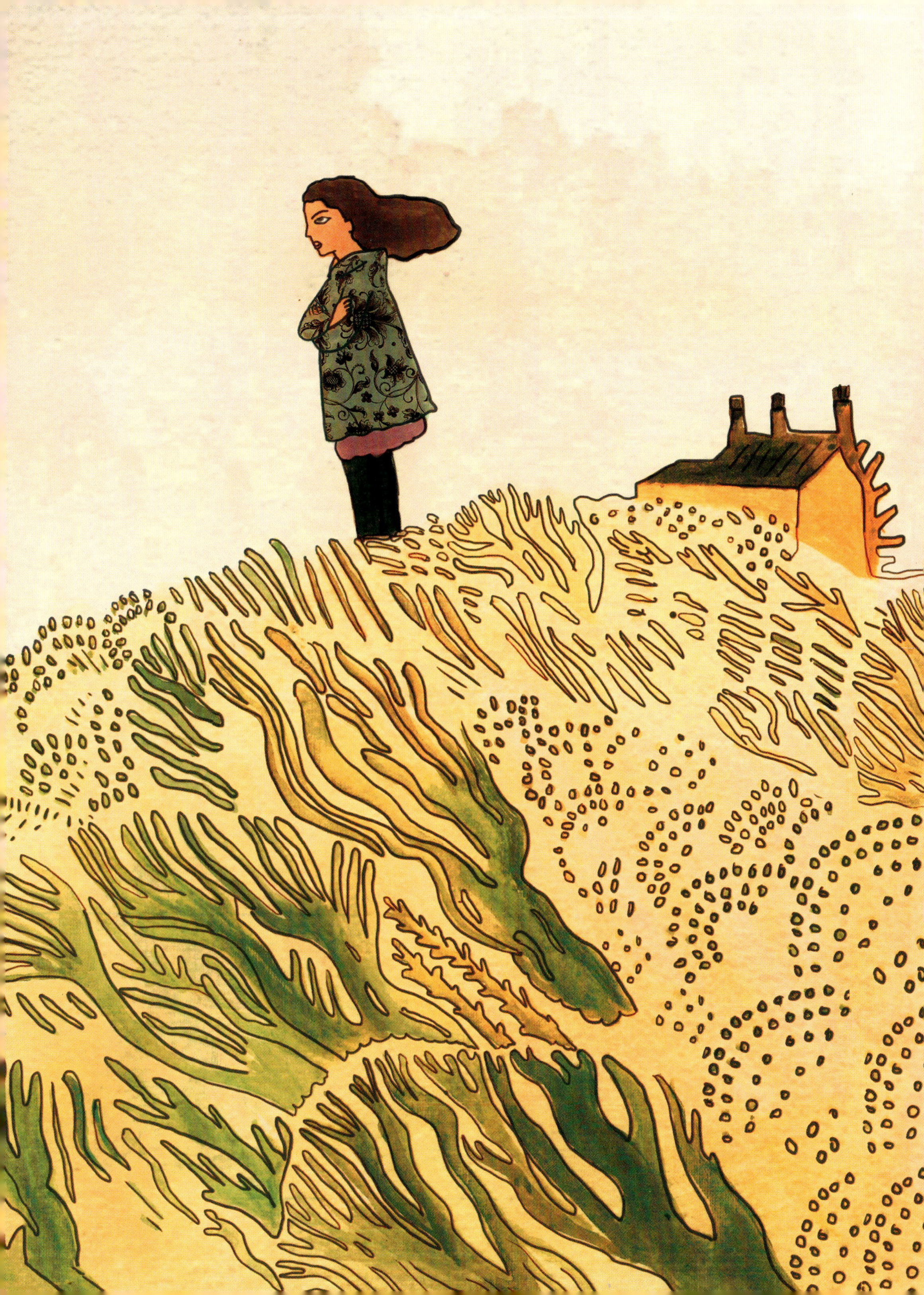

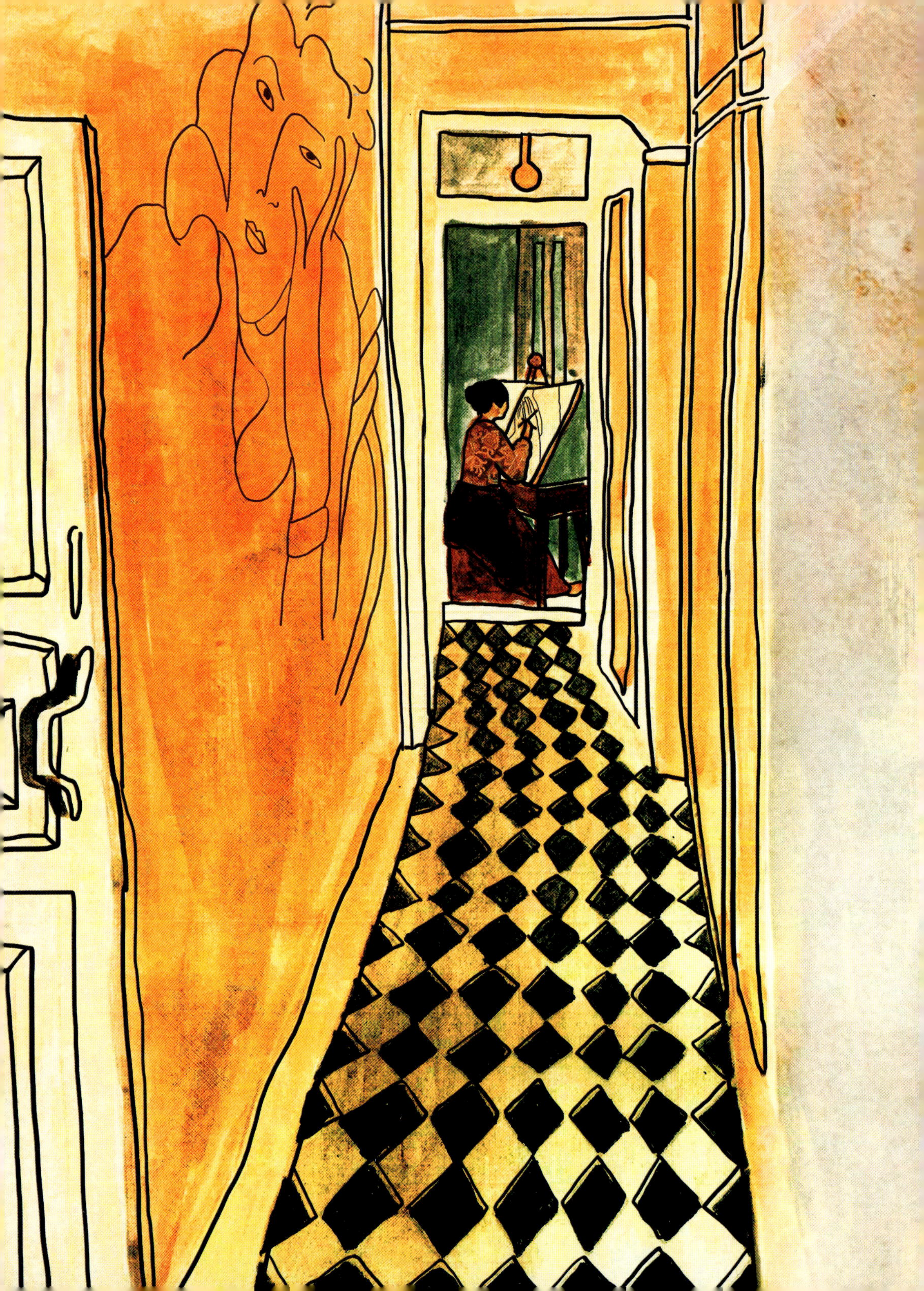

Unlike most children her age, twelve-year-old Amrita now painted women in unusual poses, with every detail of womanhood.

Her art was as unashamed and fearless as herself.

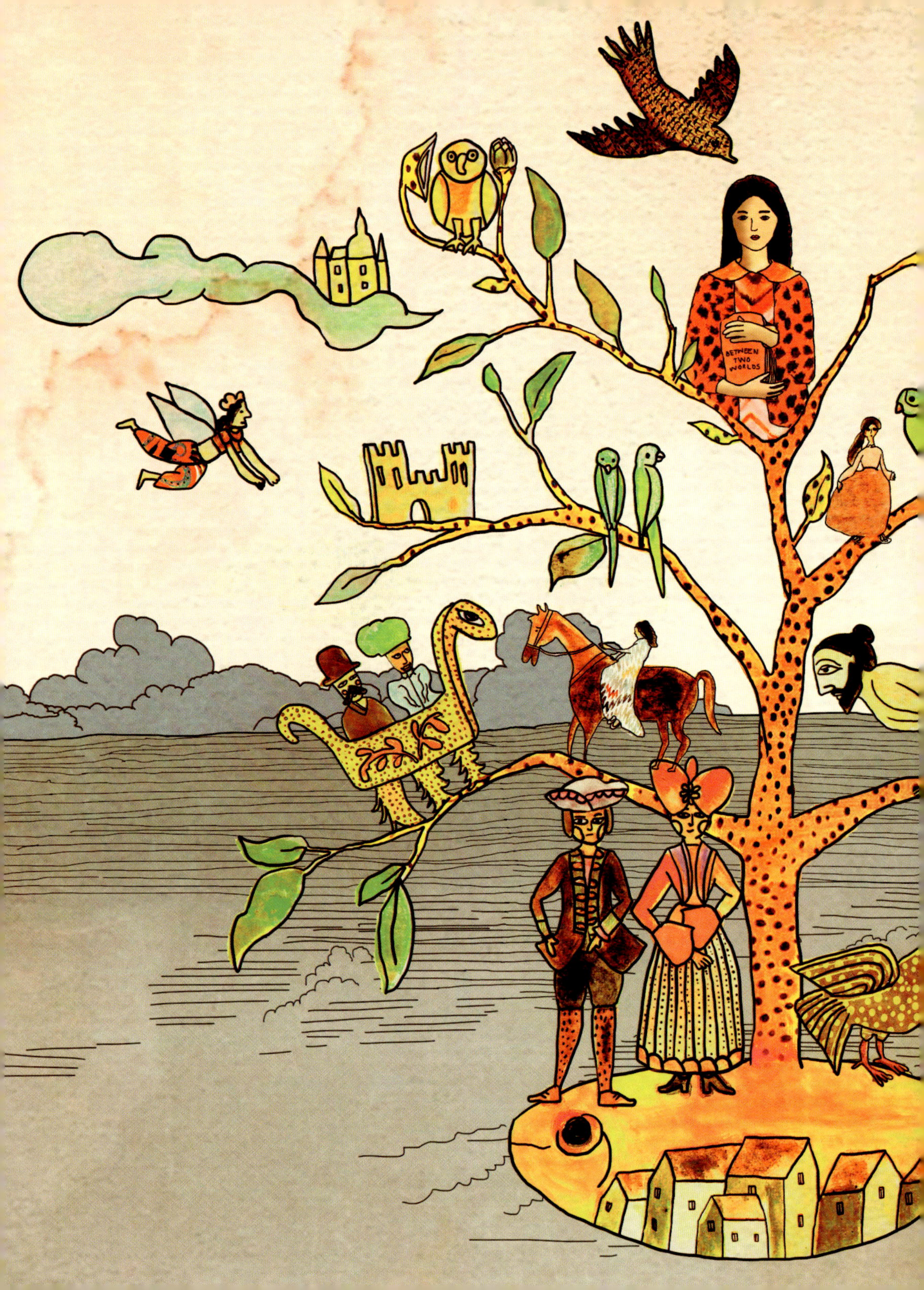
BETWEEN TWO WORLDS

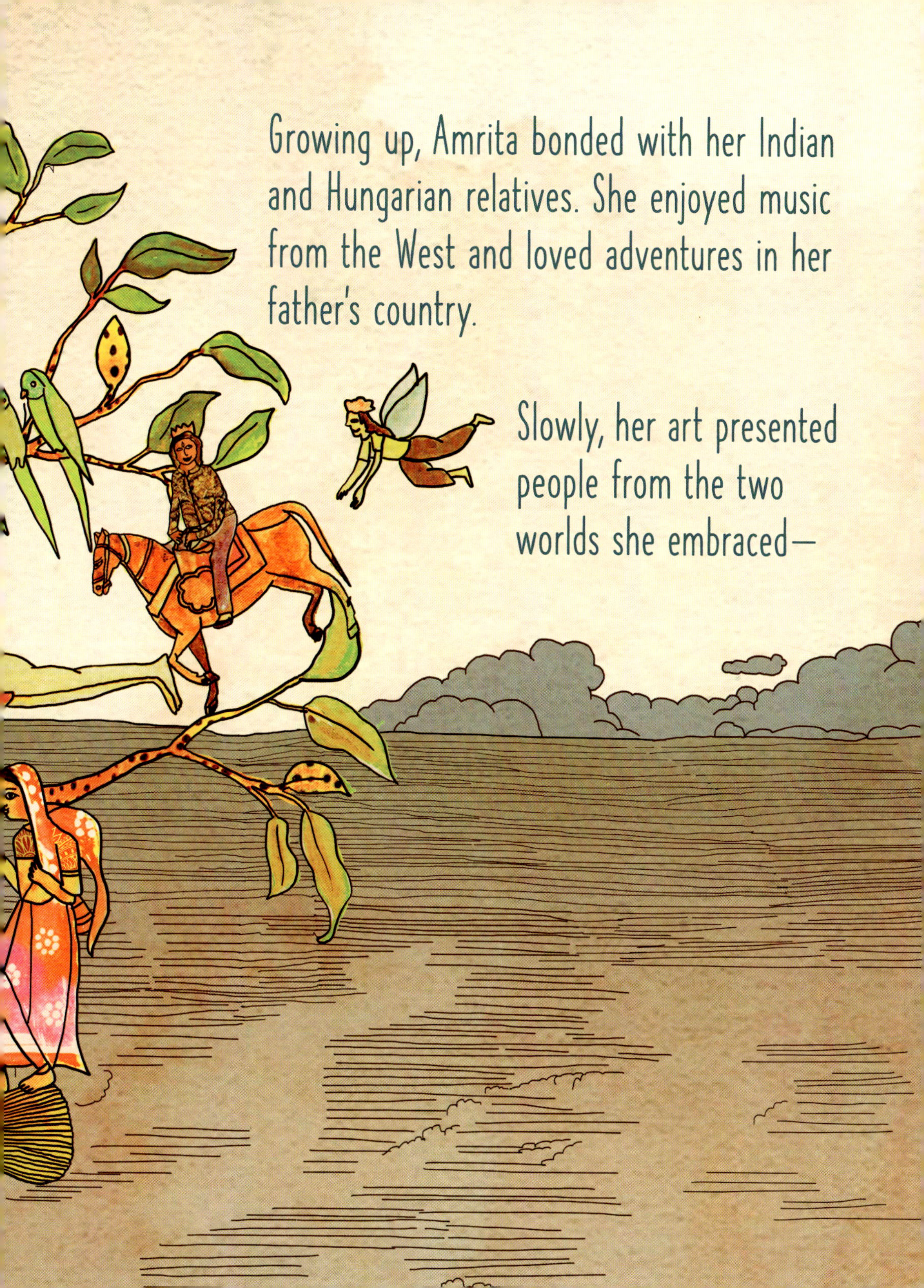

Growing up, Amrita bonded with her Indian and Hungarian relatives. She enjoyed music from the West and loved adventures in her father's country.

Slowly, her art presented people from the two worlds she embraced—

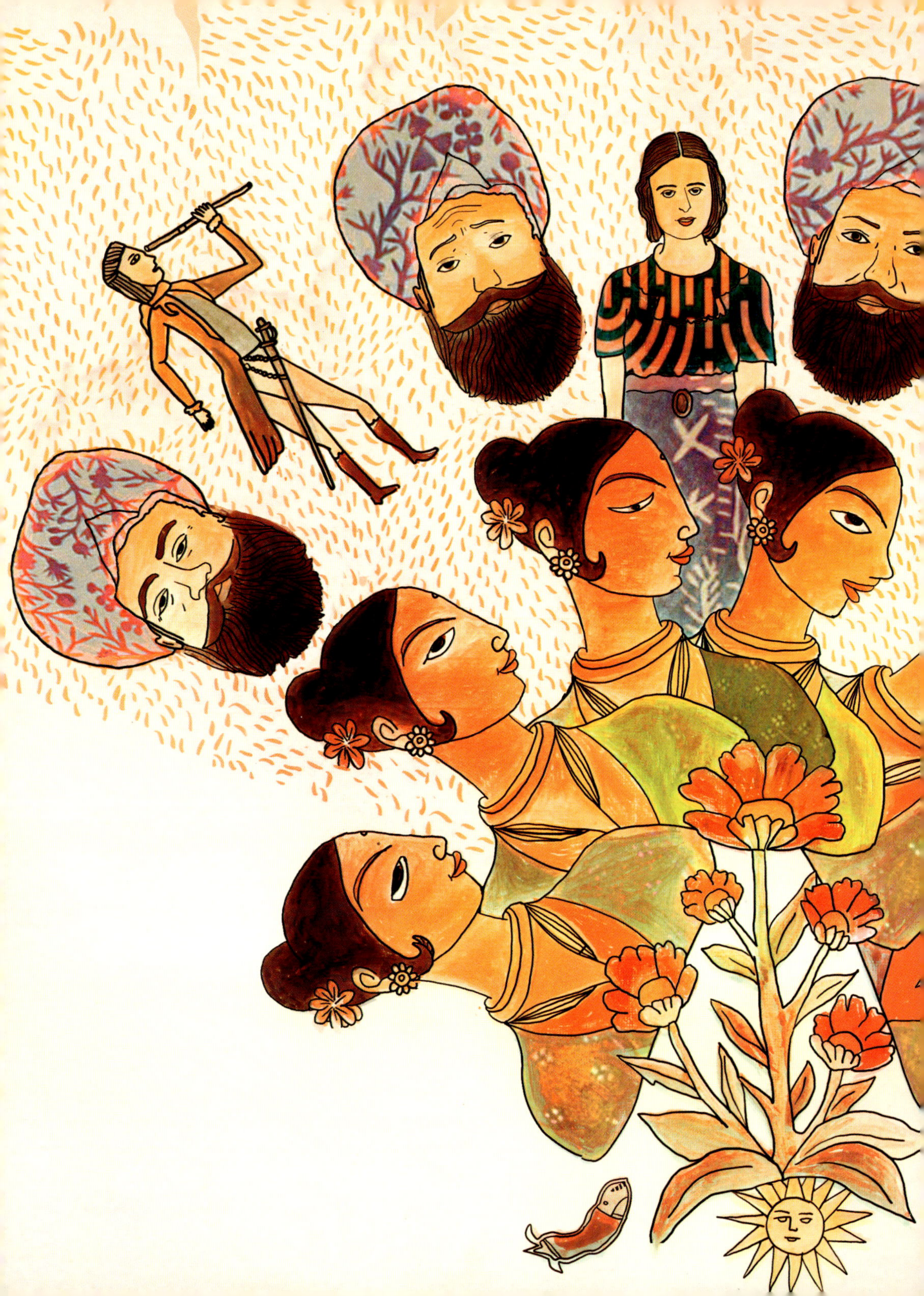

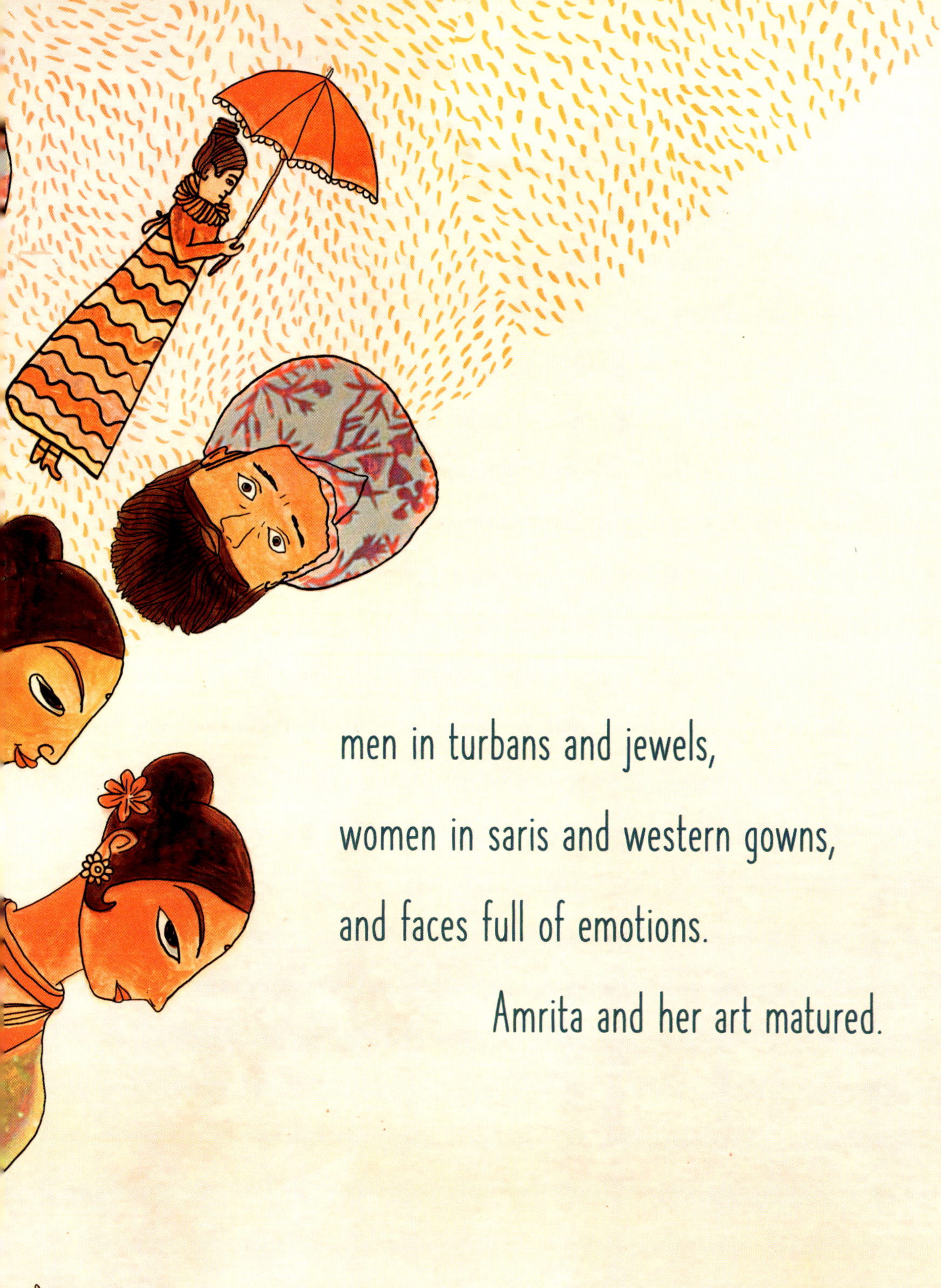

men in turbans and jewels,

women in saris and western gowns,

and faces full of emotions.

Amrita and her art matured.

By now her family insisted she study art. And so, when Amrita turned sixteen, they moved again to Europe.

For five years, Amrita flooded their Parisian flat with canvases, oil colors, and brushstrokes. She trained with a mentor who helped her explore and experiment.

In dimly lit cafes, studios, and in open spaces, she painted—

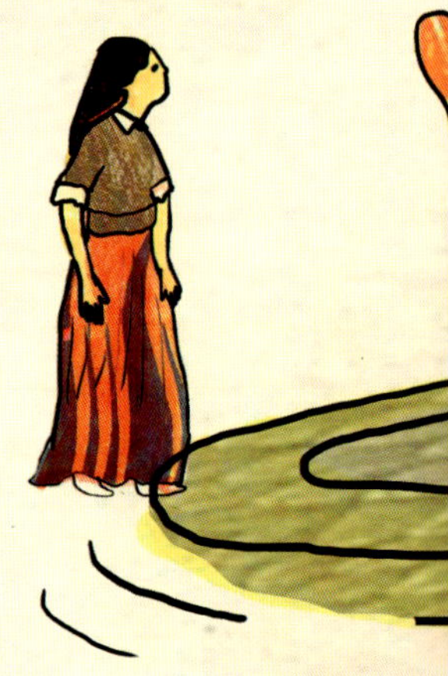

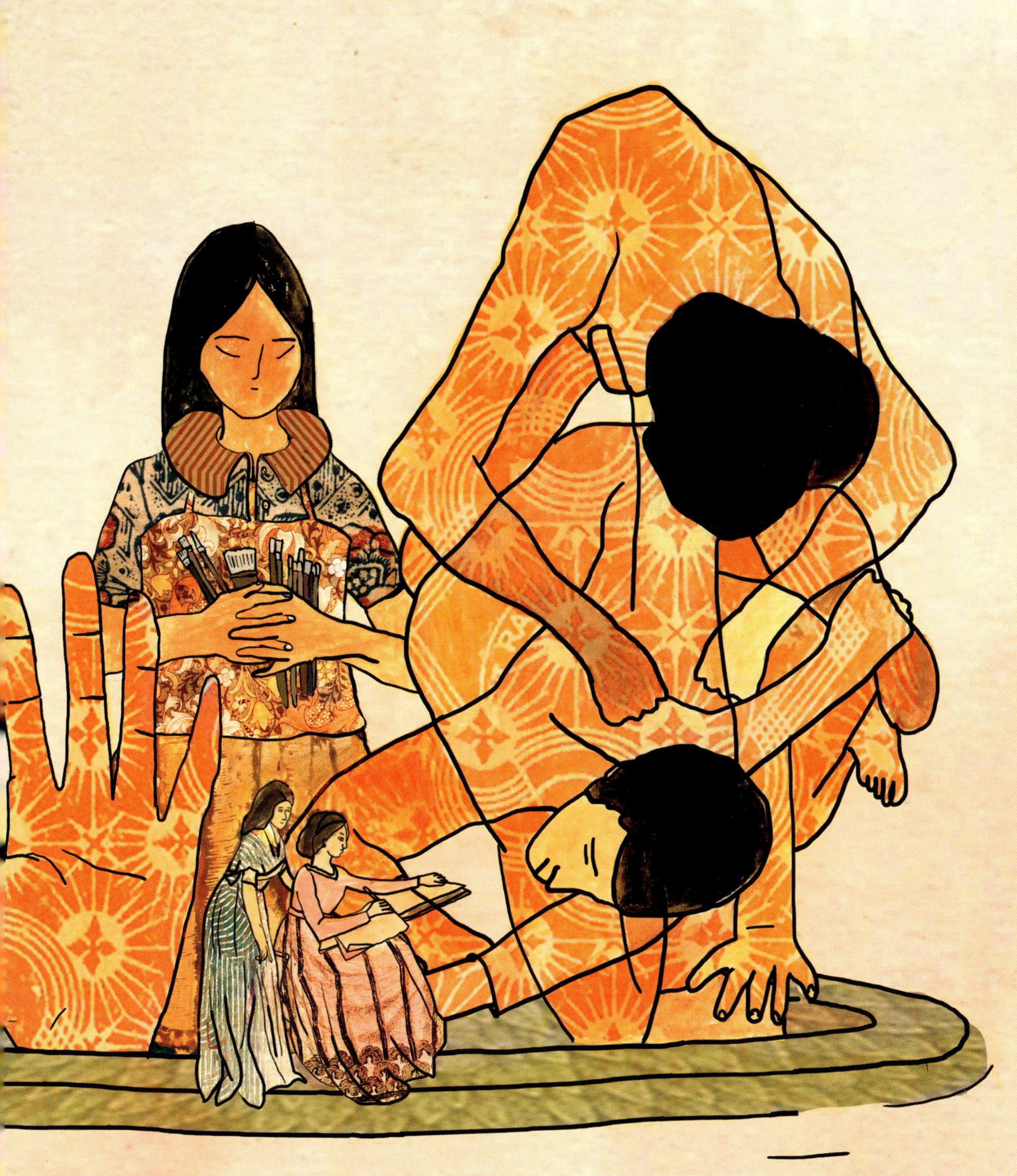

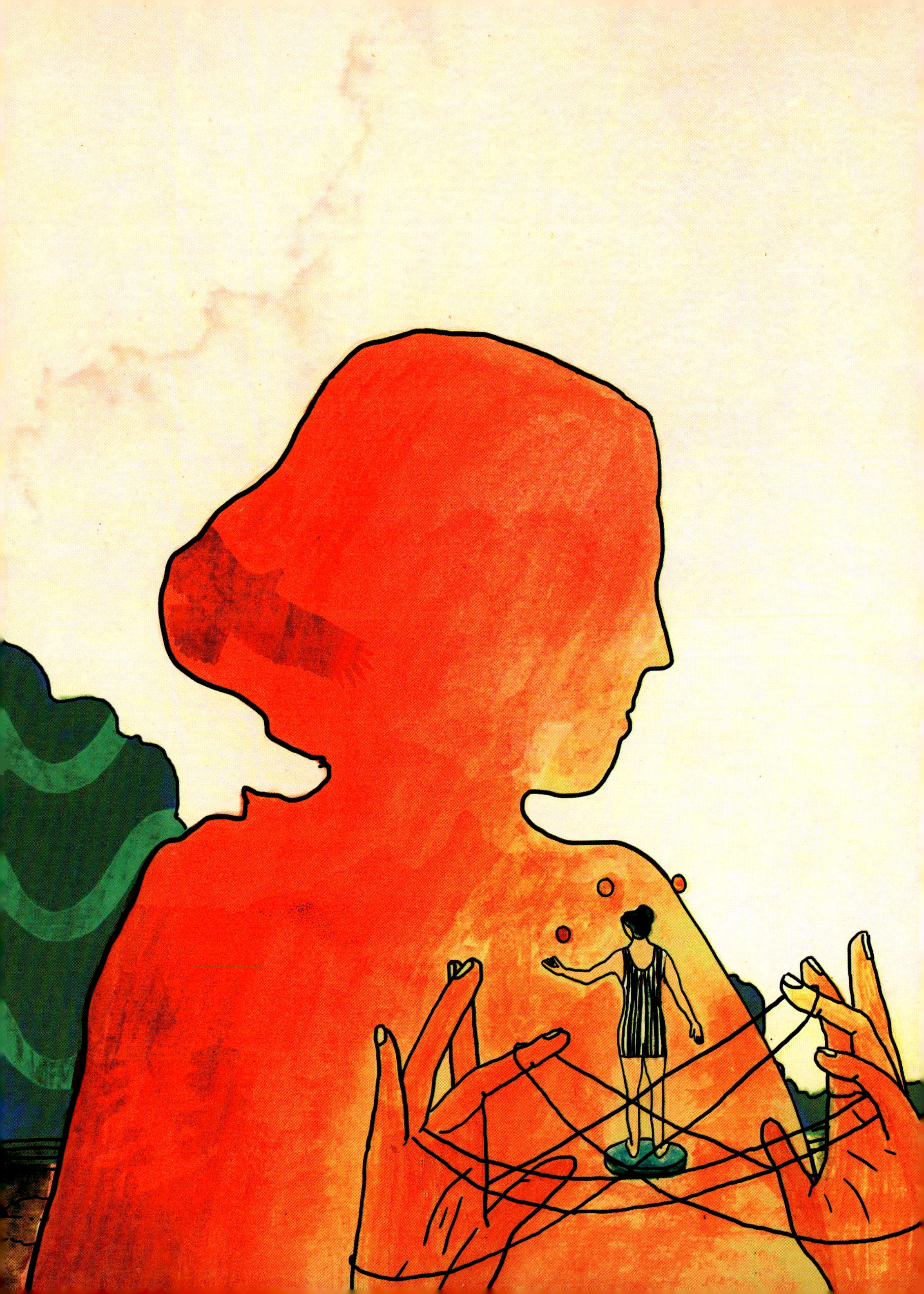

self-portraits that held secrets,

portraits of friends and models,

and bodies, not just white, but in several shades of brown.

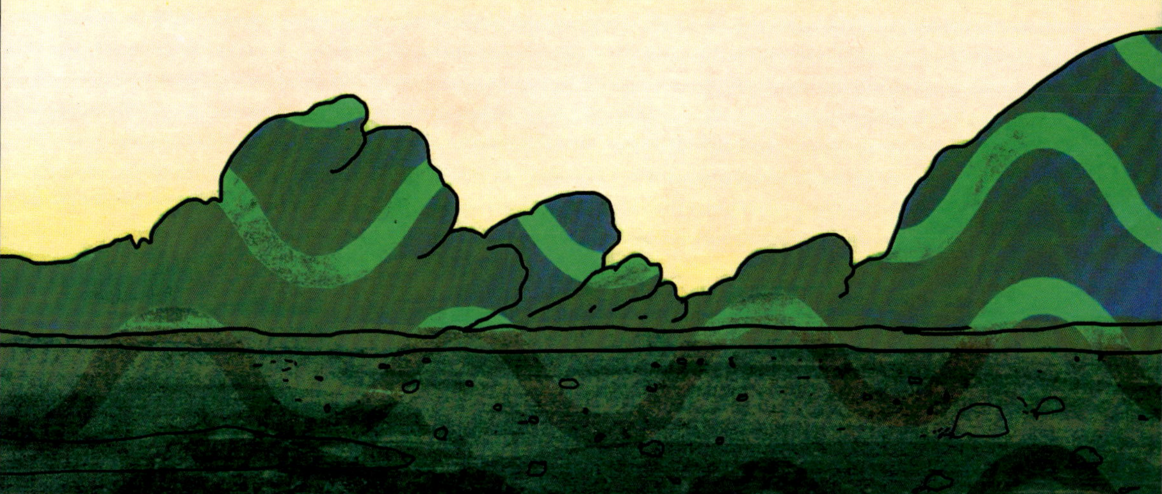

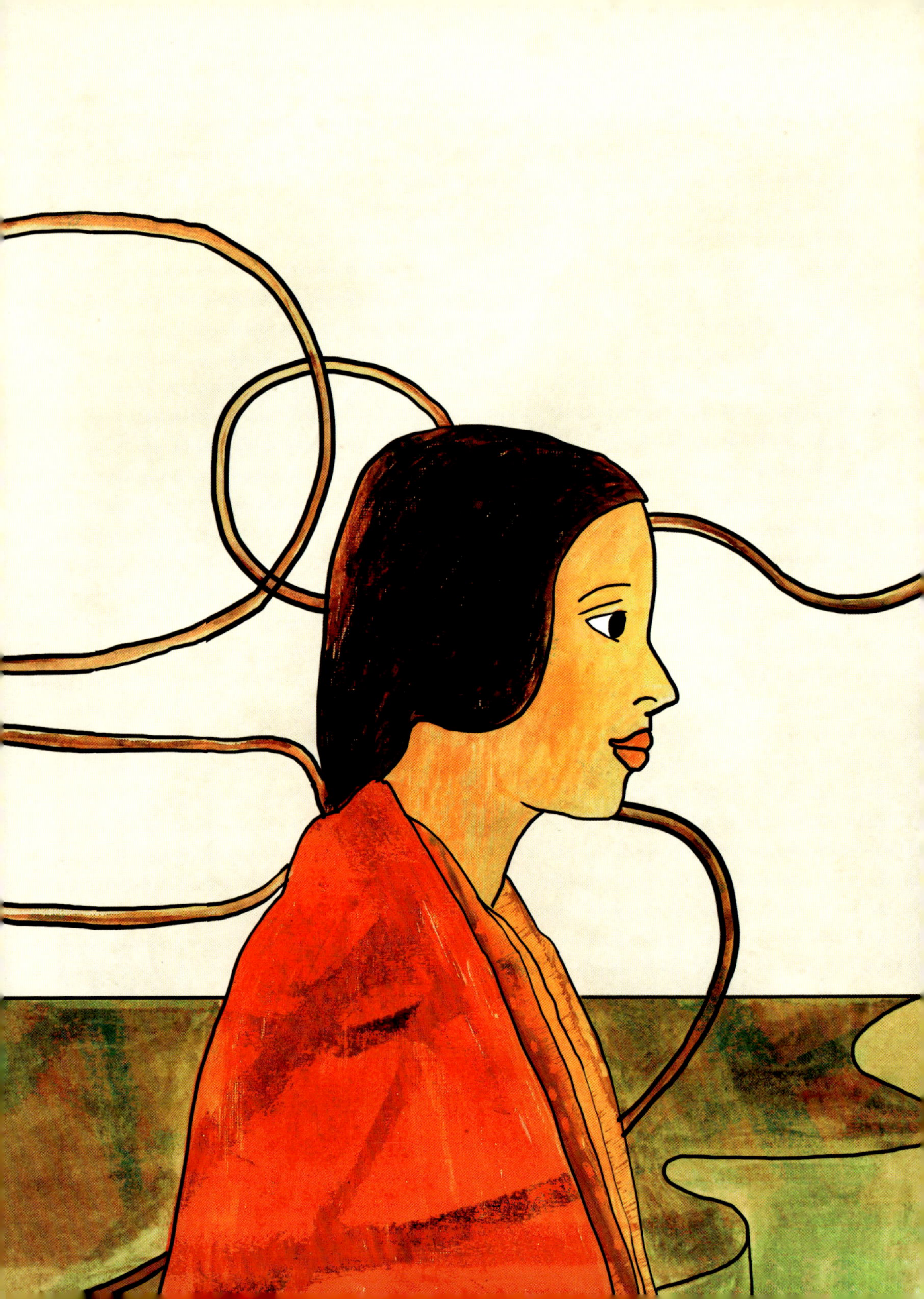

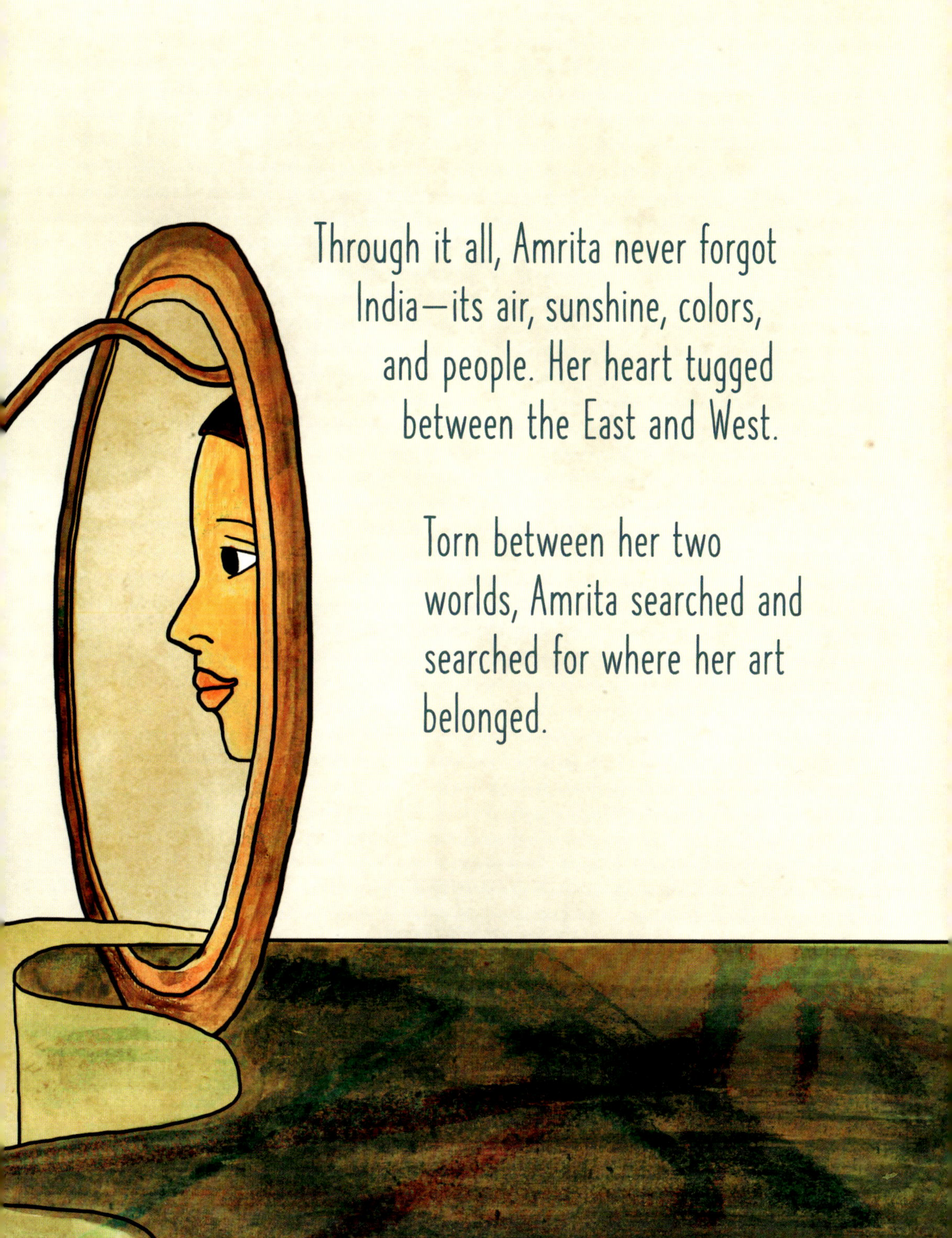

Through it all, Amrita never forgot India—its air, sunshine, colors, and people. Her heart tugged between the East and West.

Torn between her two worlds, Amrita searched and searched for where her art belonged.

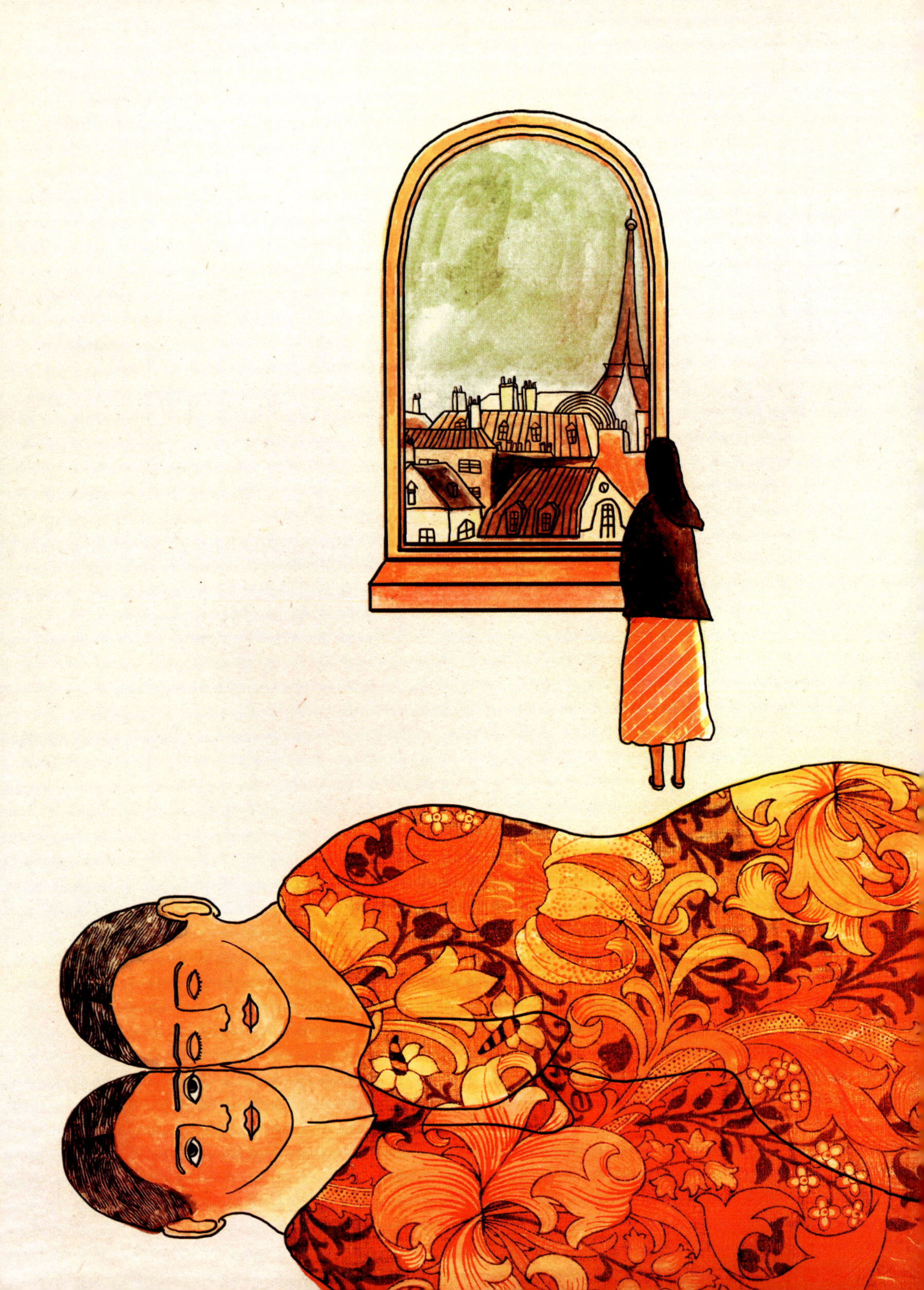

Soon, she grew restless in Paris that was seeped in cold blues. And longed to paint something new.

India was calling her from across the sea.

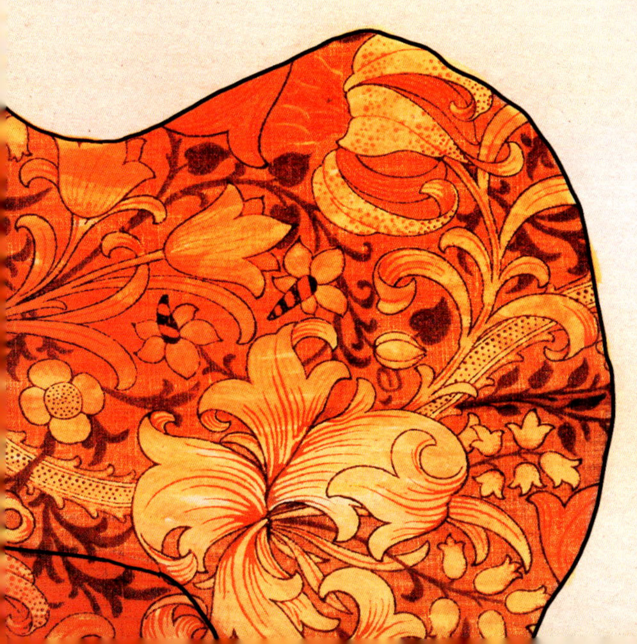

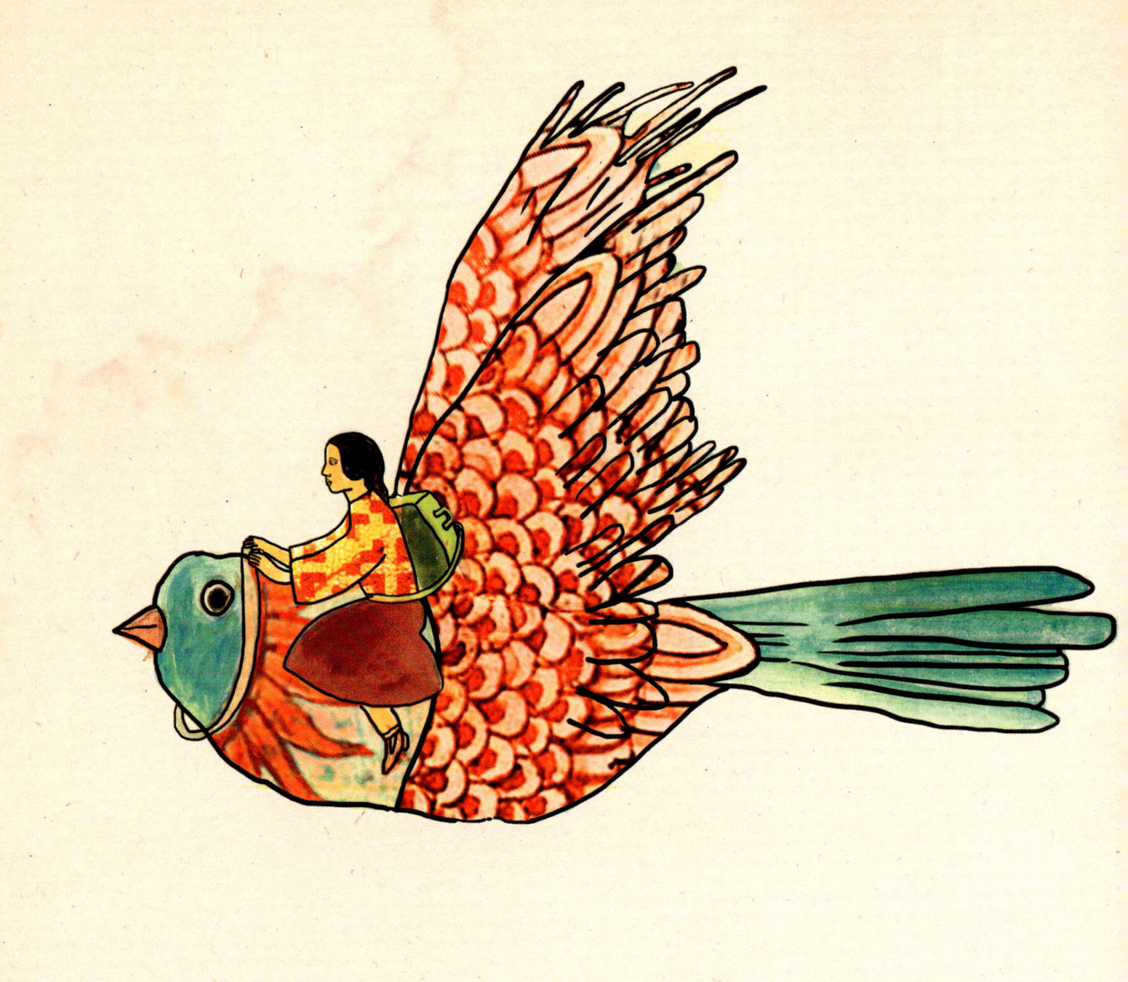

At twenty-one, Amrita set sail again.

With every move, she learned more about herself and her art.

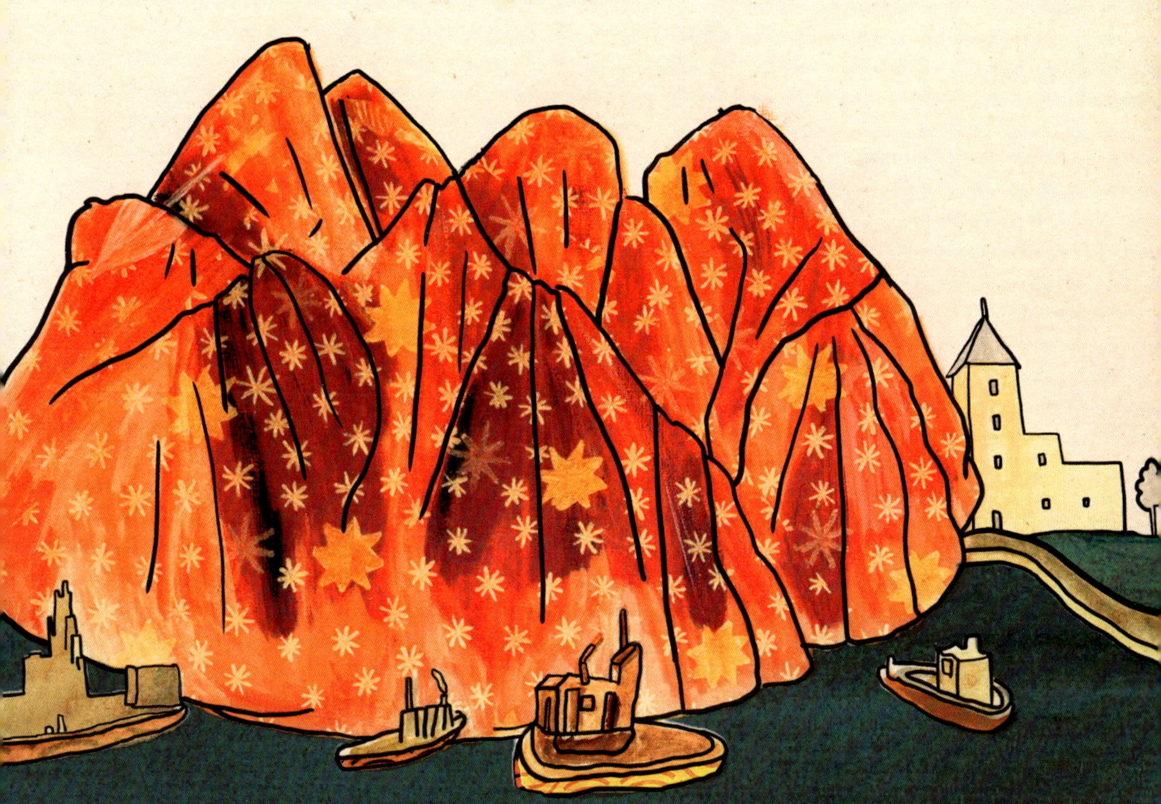

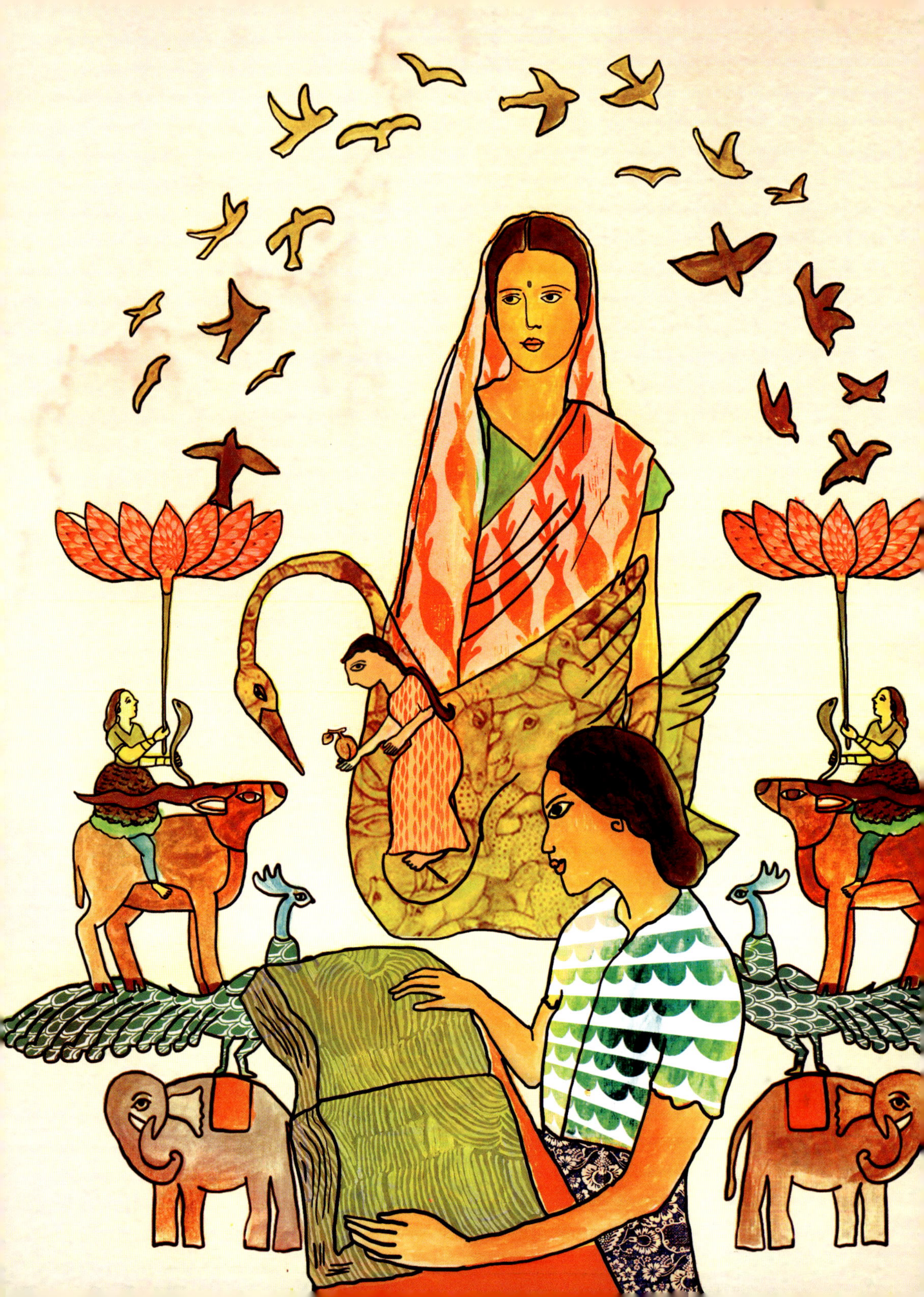

In India,

she could breathe.

She could wander.

She could create from her heart again.

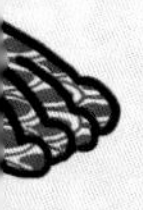

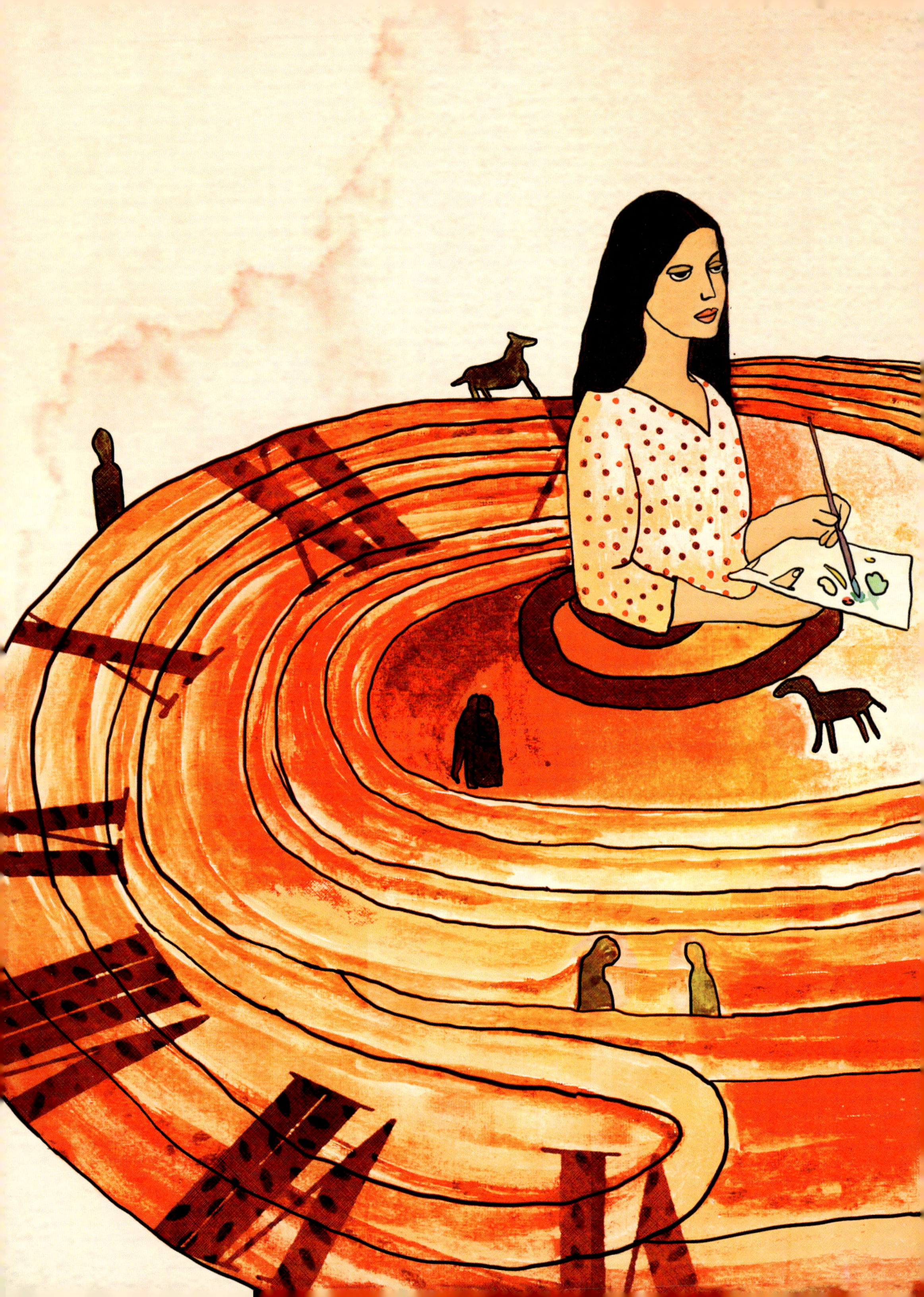

At a time of few women artists, Amrita mixed bold colors and stroked them on canvases.

She used all she had learned in Europe and painted an India no one else dared. Like looking into a mirror, Amrita searched the faces of lonely women and bored workers, fruit vendors and village folks. She found her art in ordinary lives.

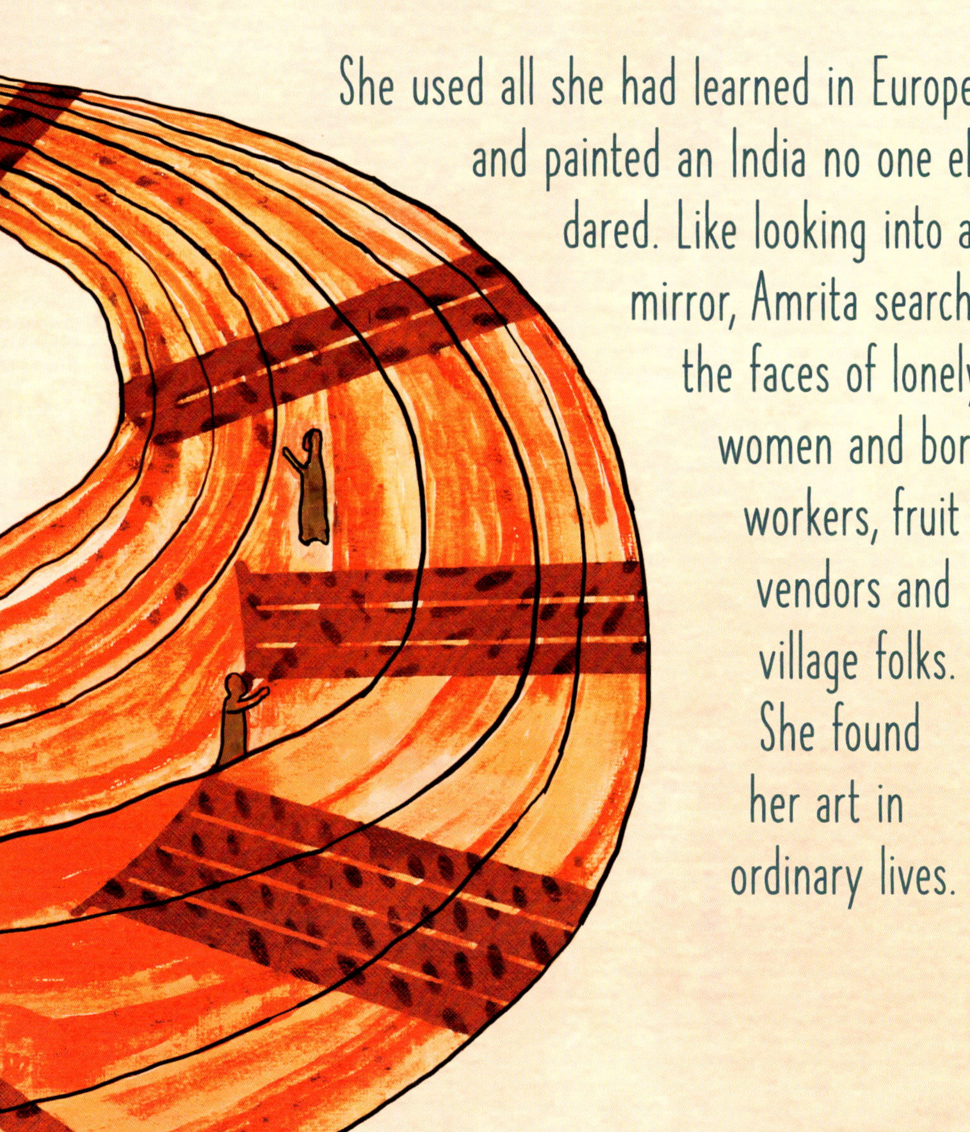

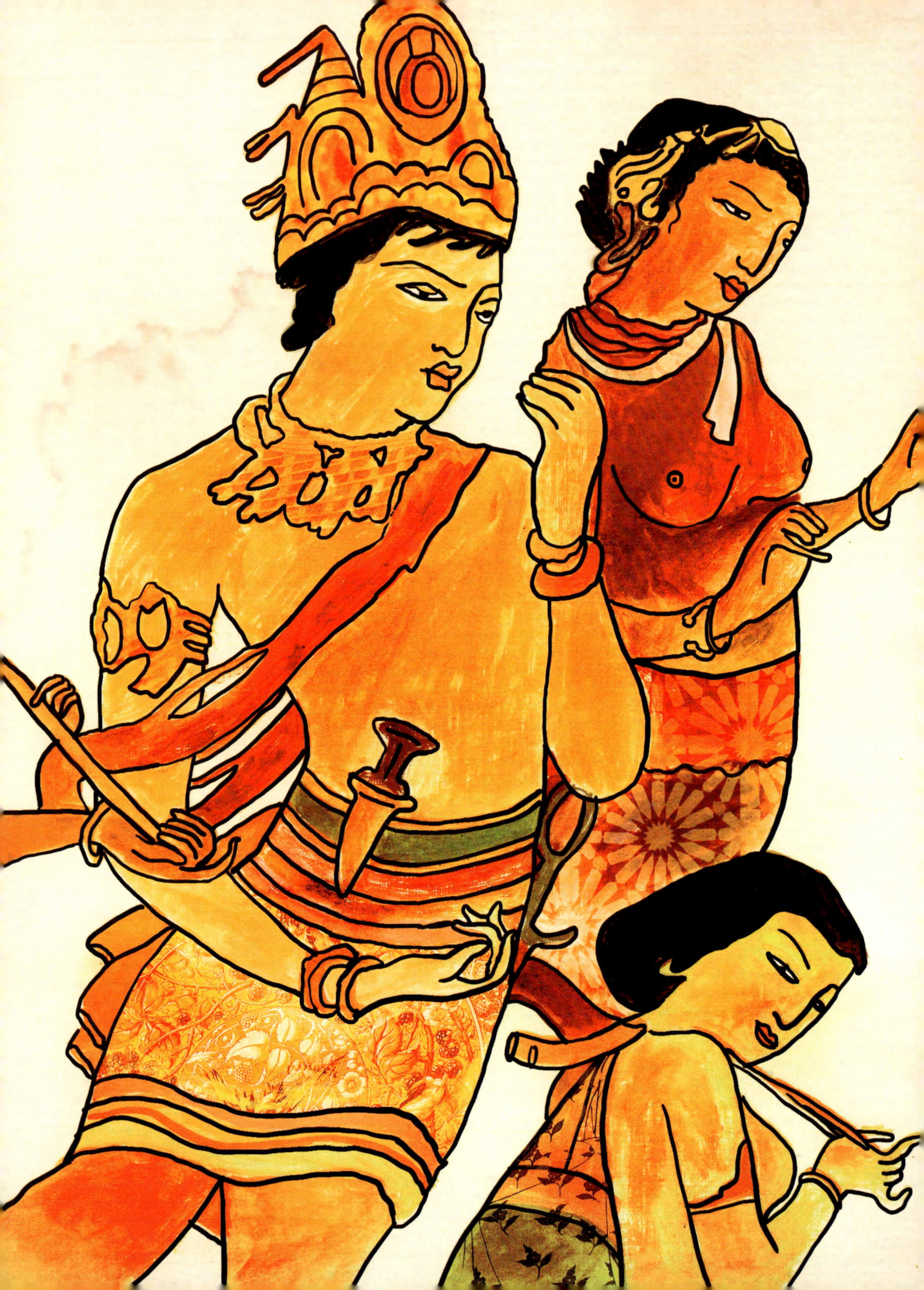

For more inspiration, she traveled to quiet towns in India.

She spent hours in front of the easel and pushed boundaries by fusing western and traditional forms.

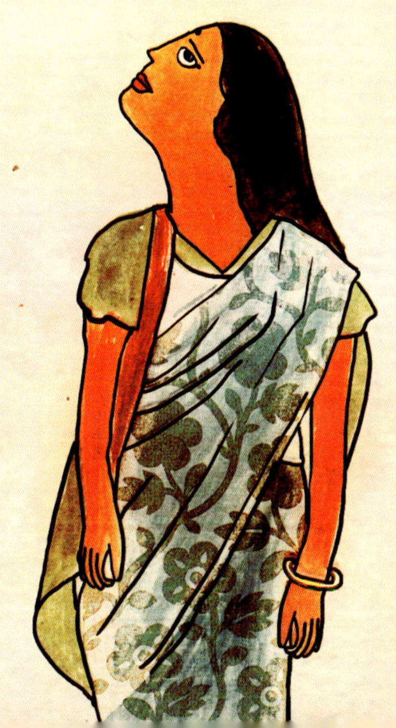

Inside galleries, many gasped in shock. Some stared and smiled. Very few carried her paintings home.

But Amrita never gave up. She only painted more.

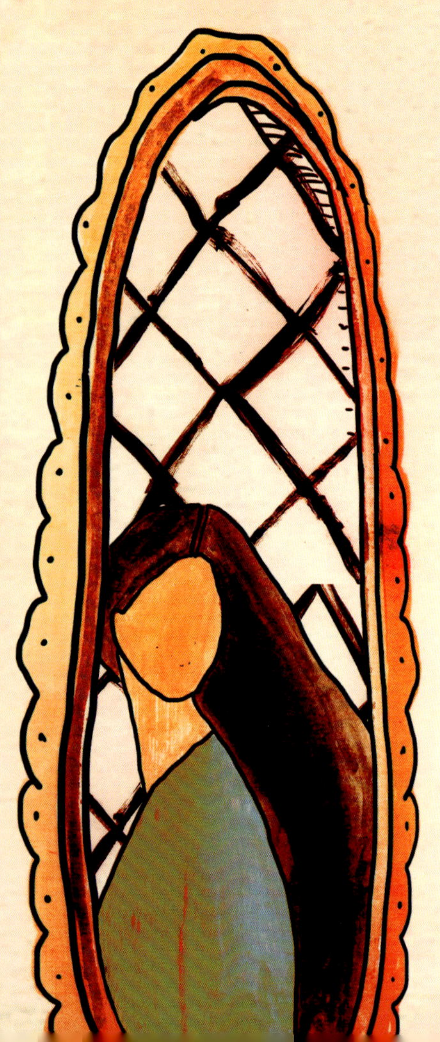

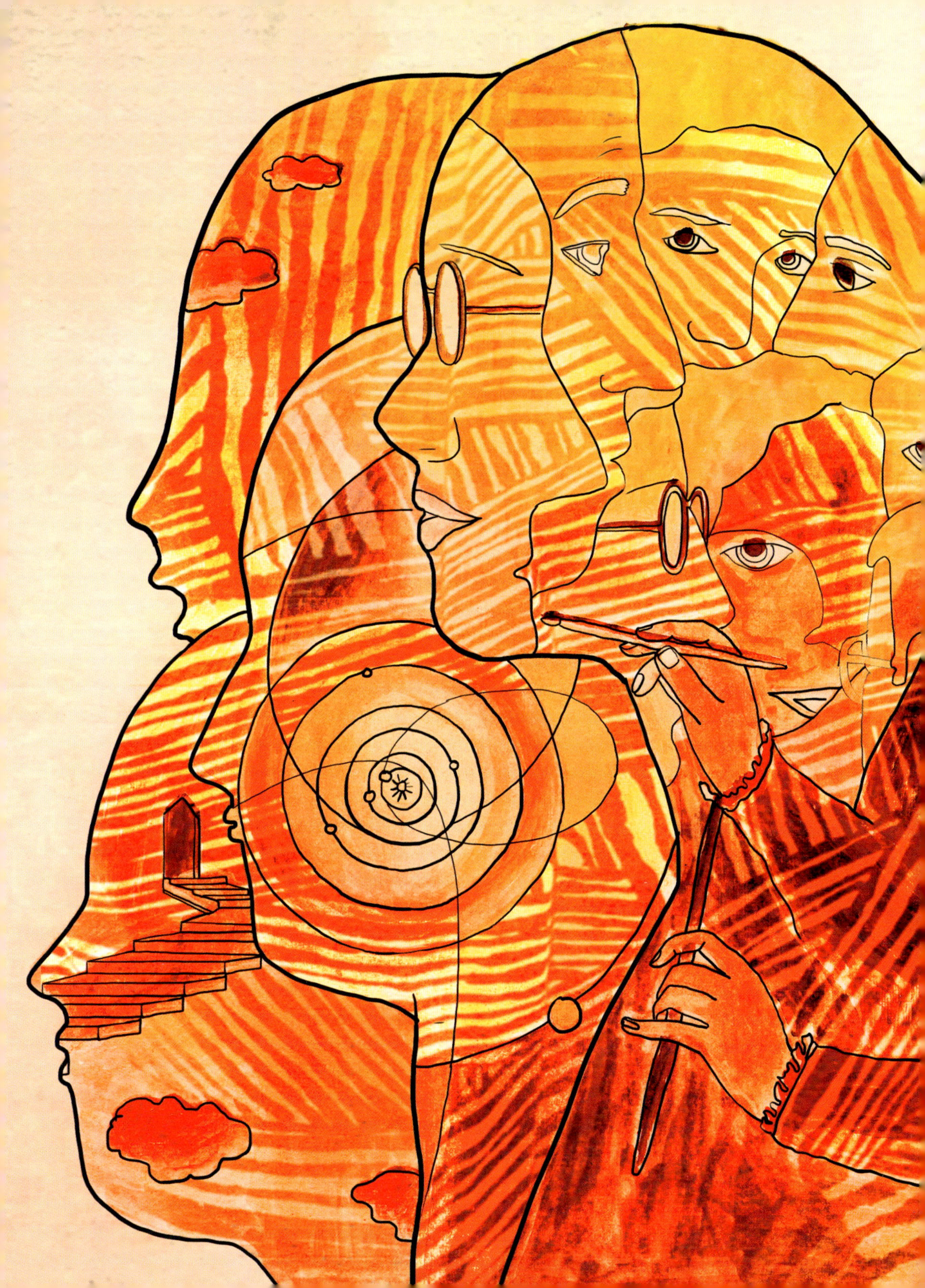

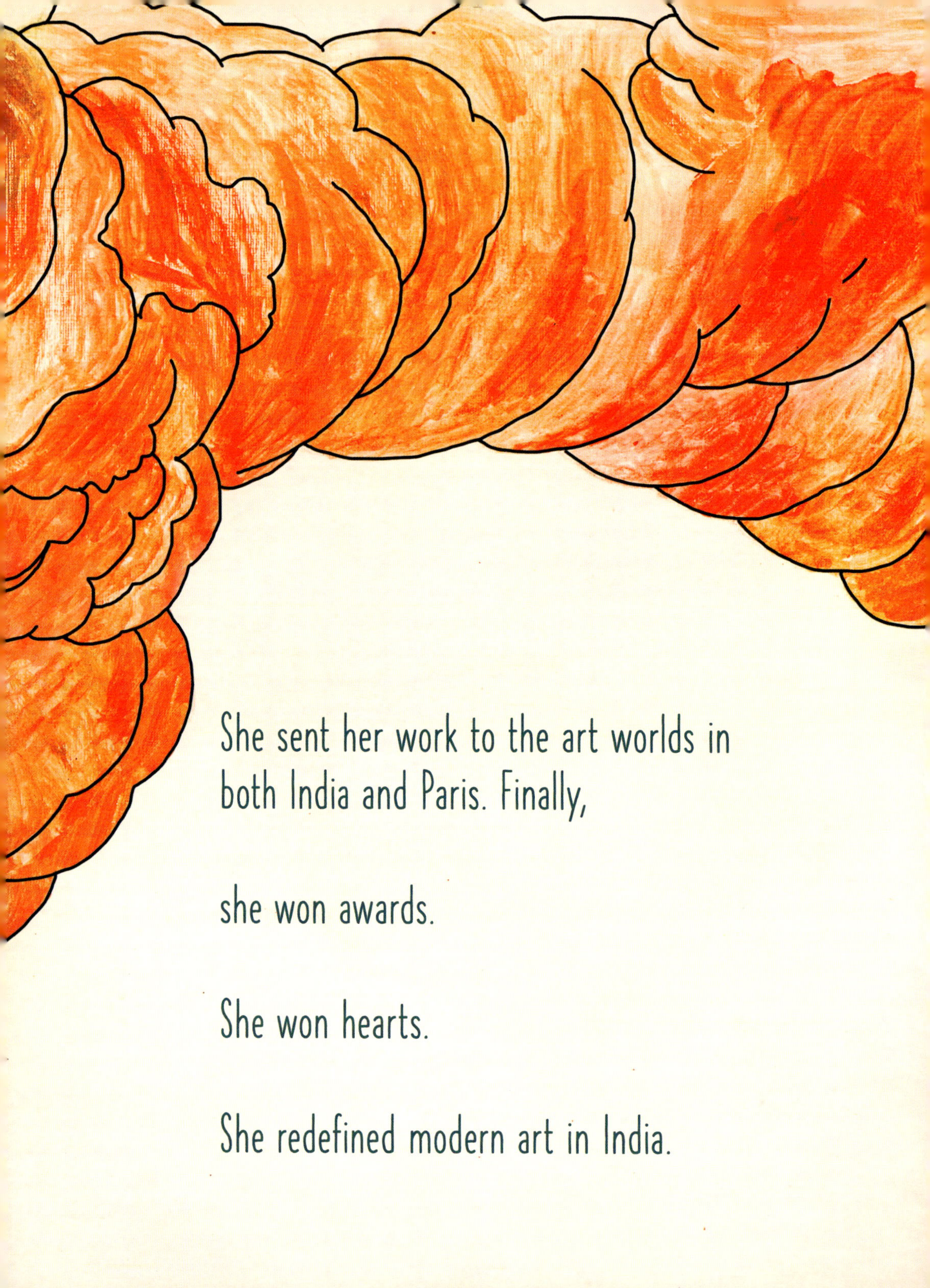

She sent her work to the art worlds in both India and Paris. Finally,

she won awards.

She won hearts.

She redefined modern art in India.

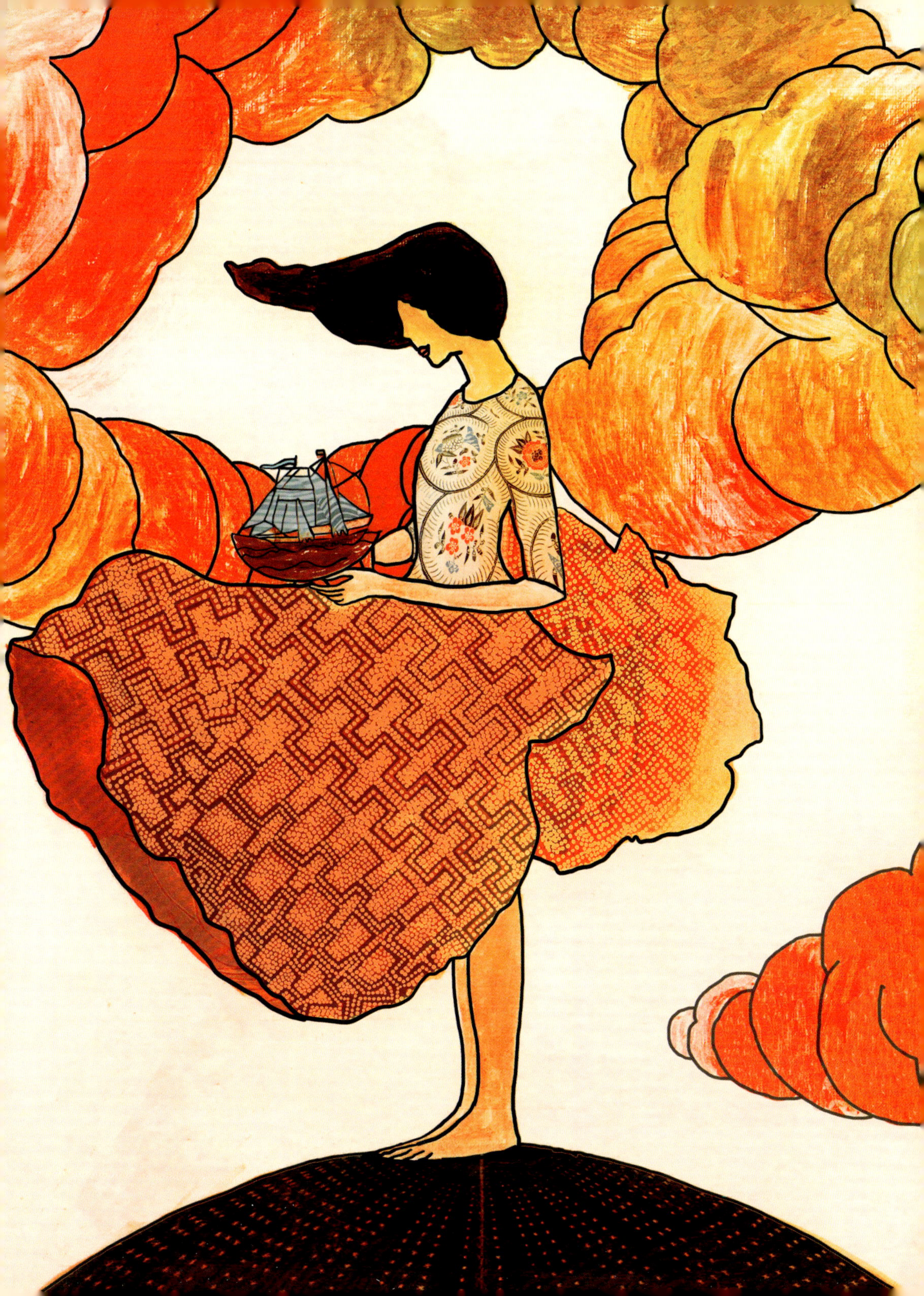

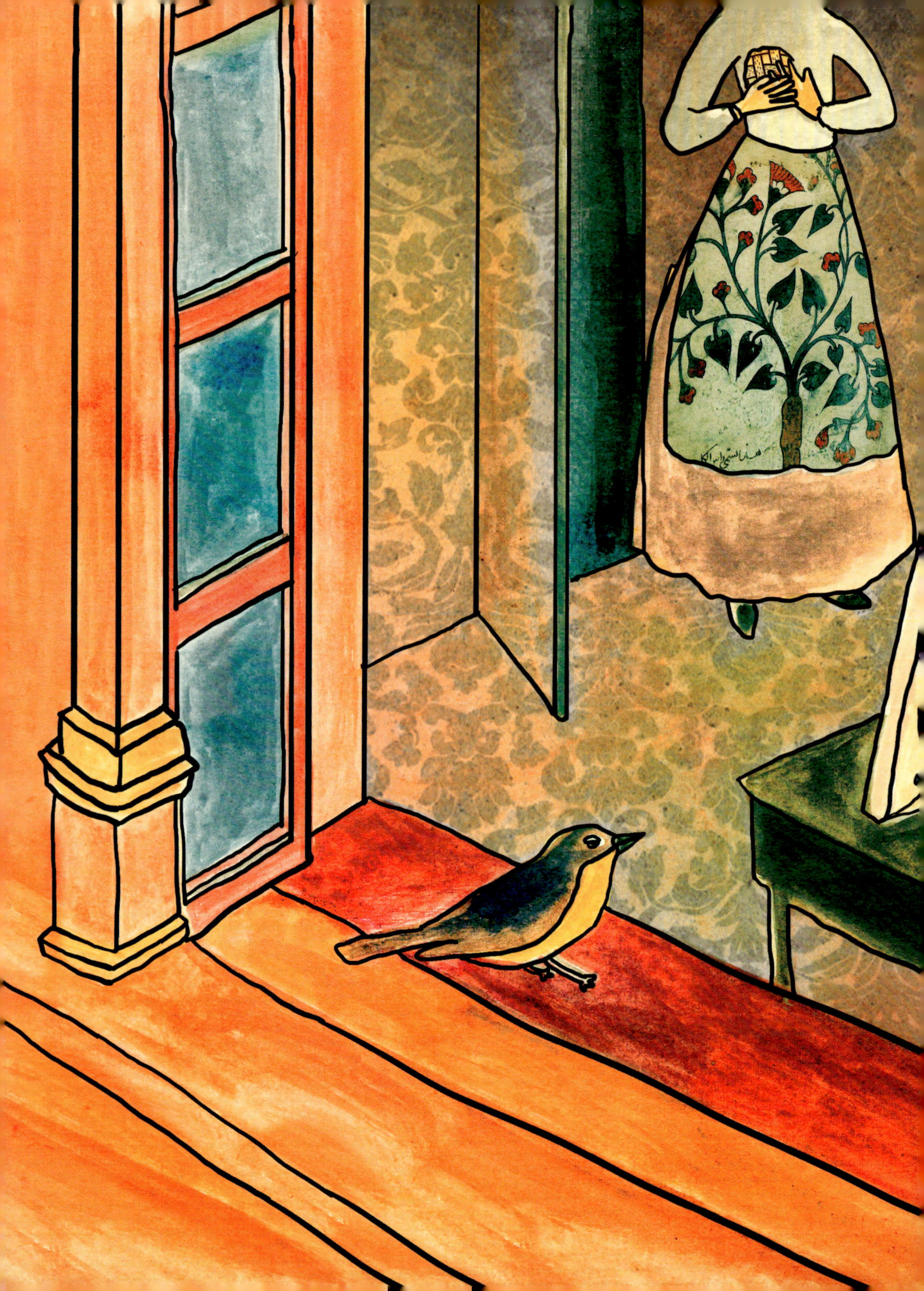

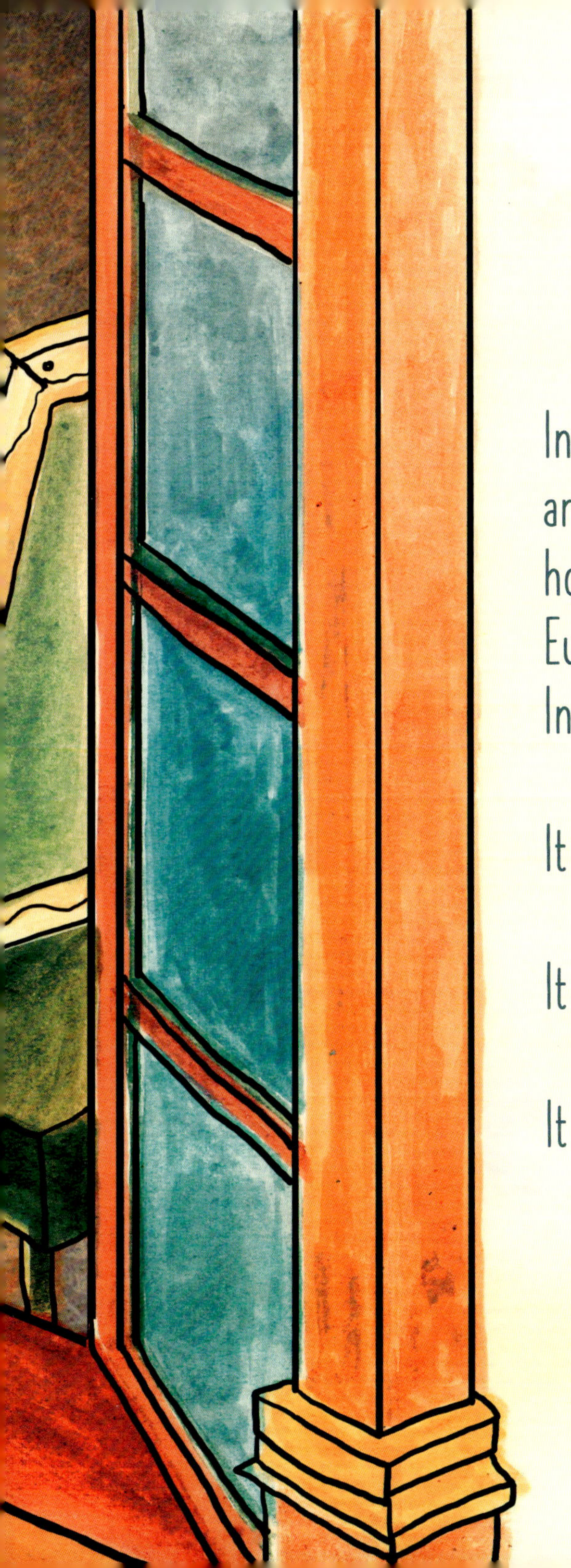

In a corner of her studio, an art canvas that depicted mud houses and buffaloes combined European techniques with rich Indian colors.

It lay unfinished.

It would remain unfinished.

It was Amrita's last work.

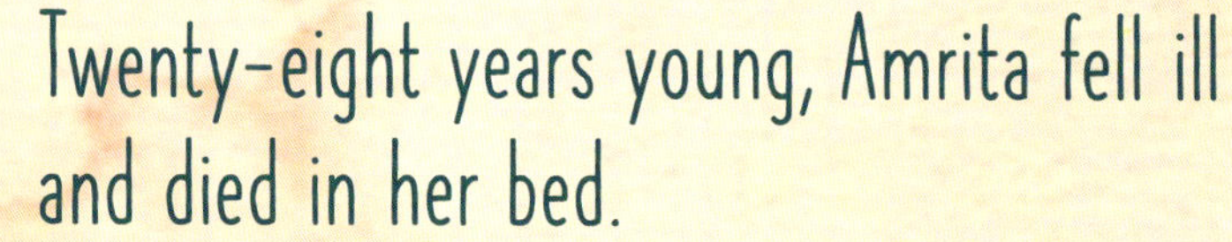

Twenty-eight years young, Amrita fell ill and died in her bed.

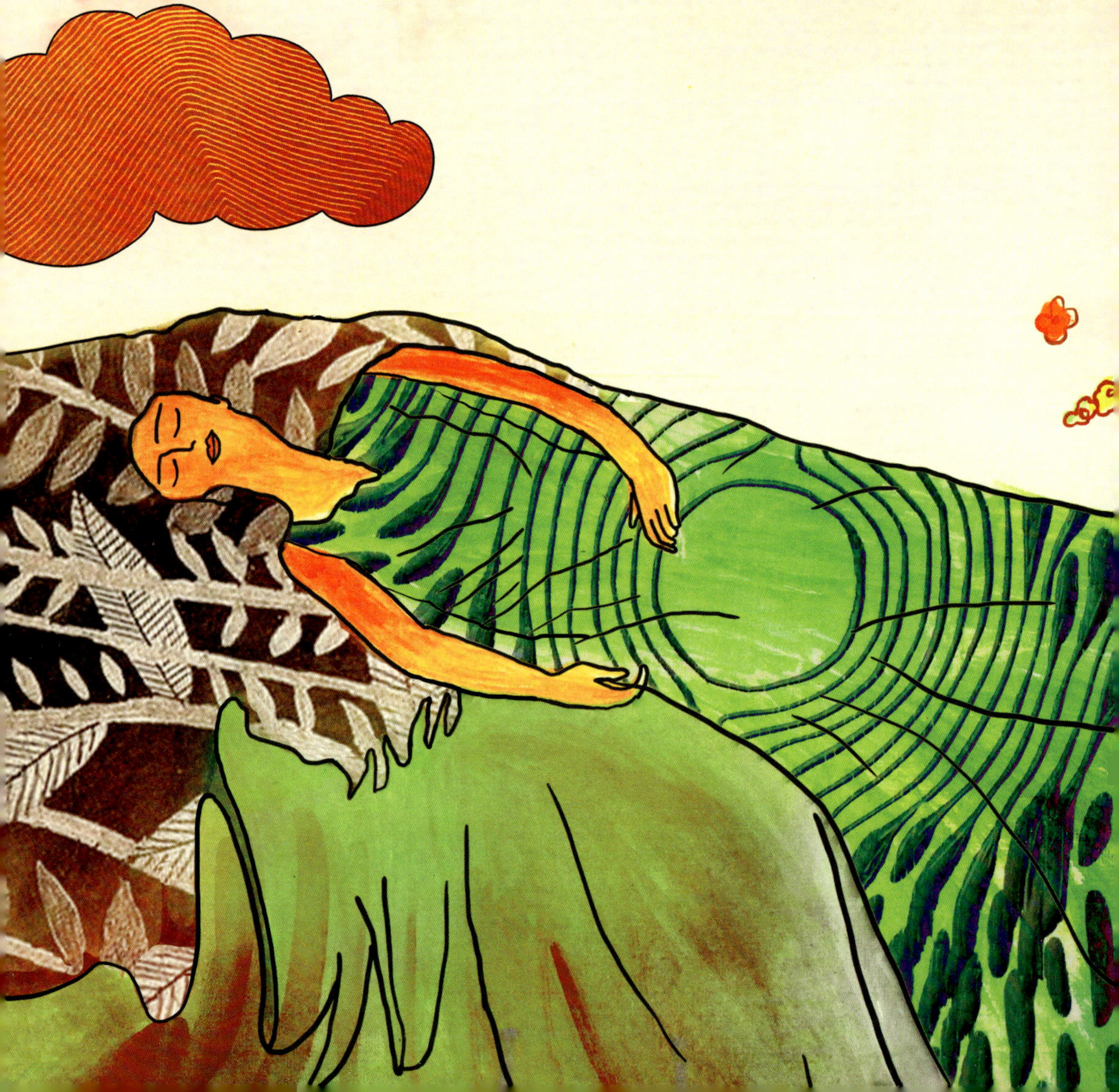

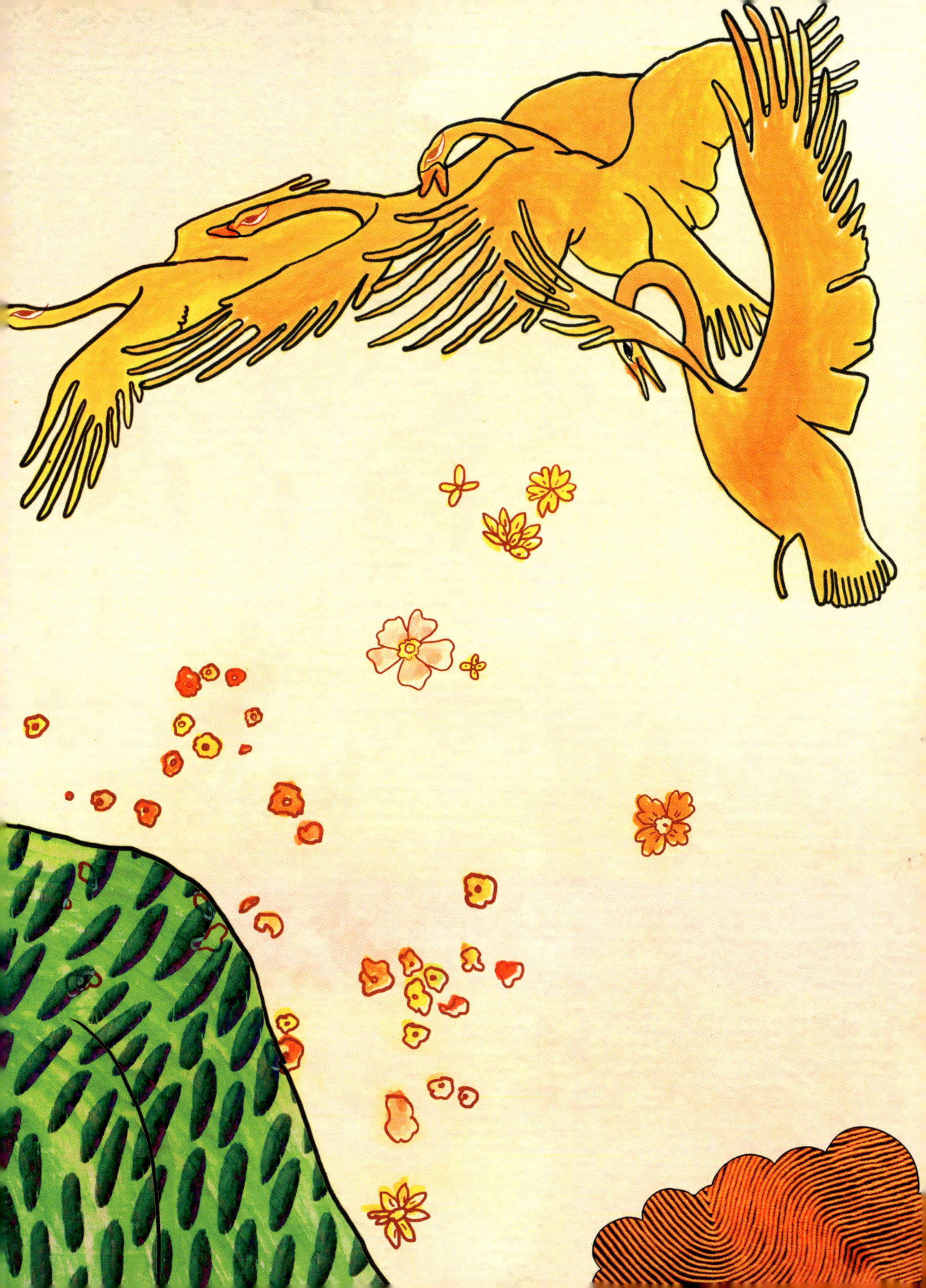

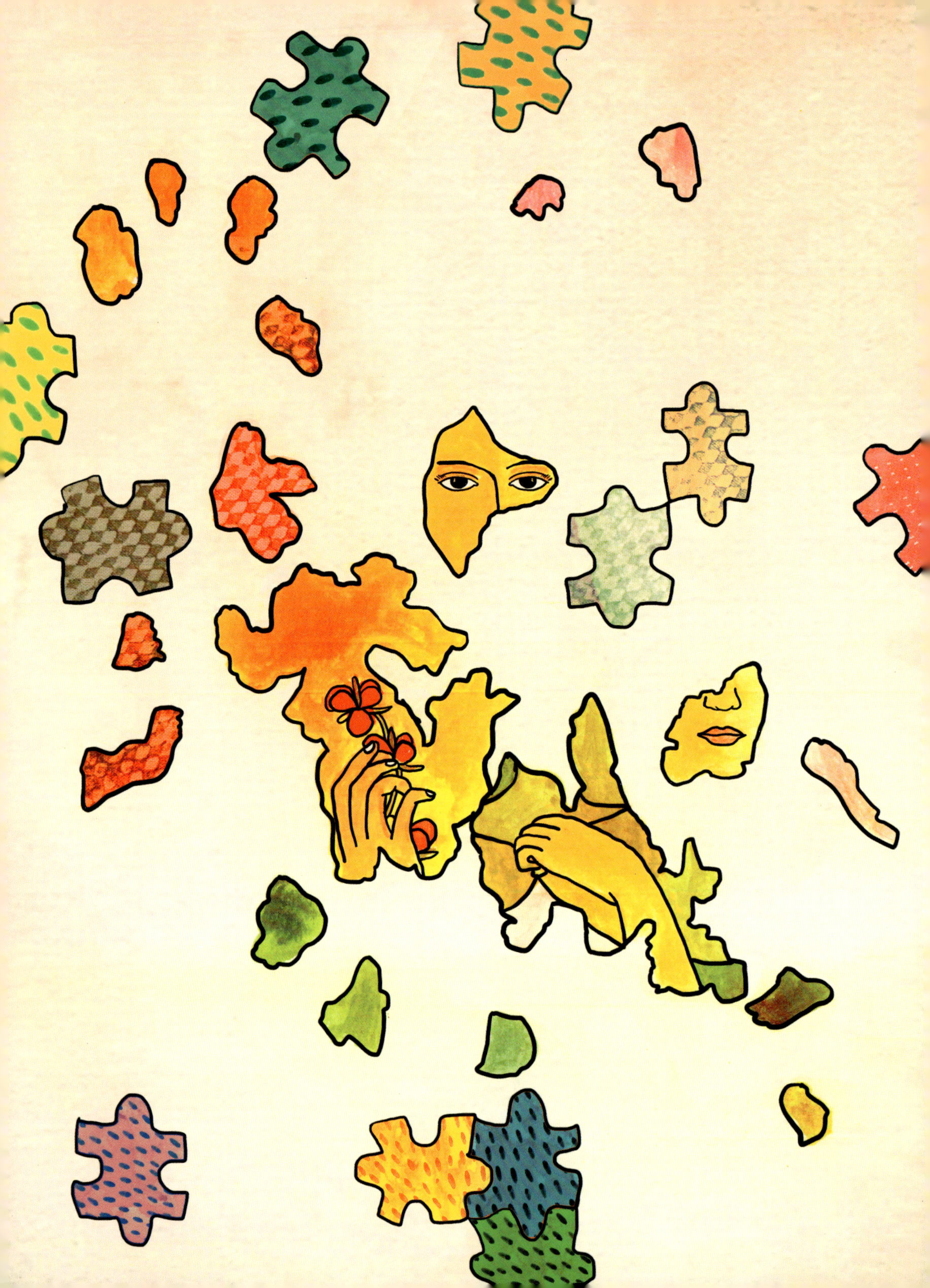

Across continents and rough seas,

from the cloudy grays of the West,

to the earthy reds of the East,

Amrita had searched and searched
and searched . . .

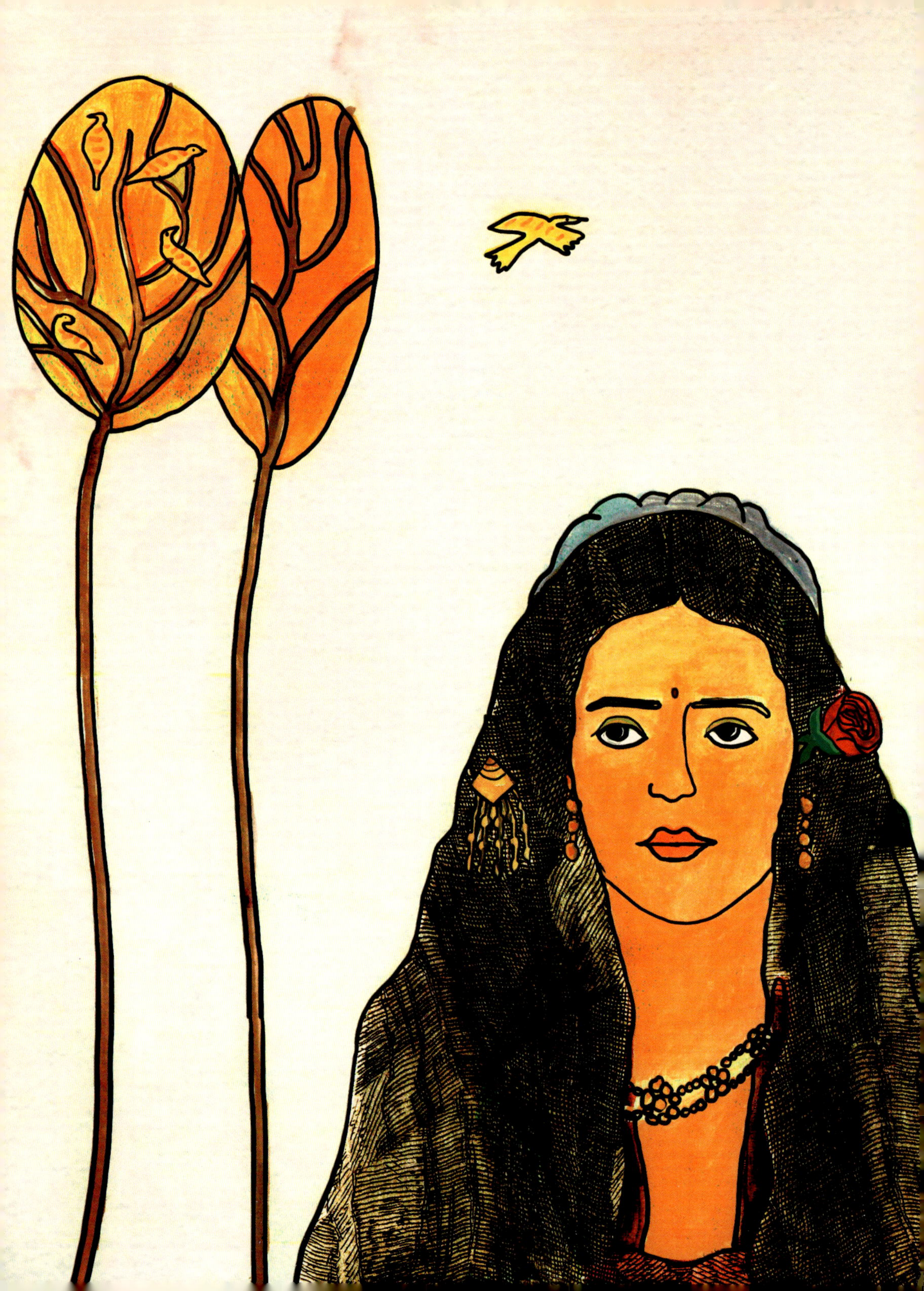

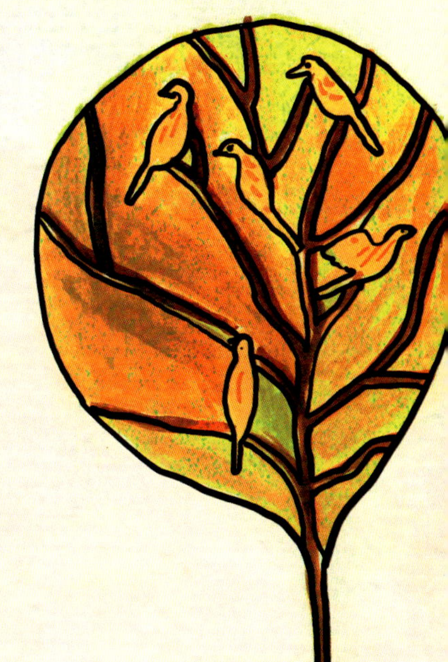

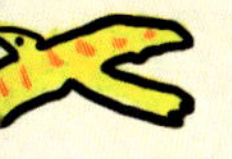

. . . until she discovered home in her own art—where her two worlds, East and West, intertwined.

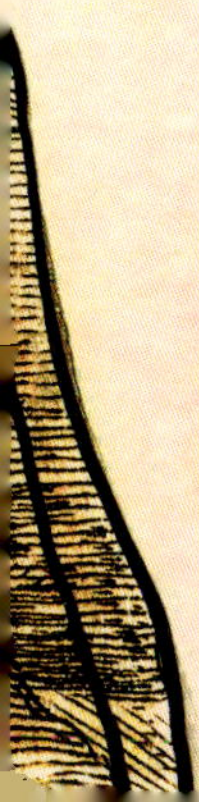

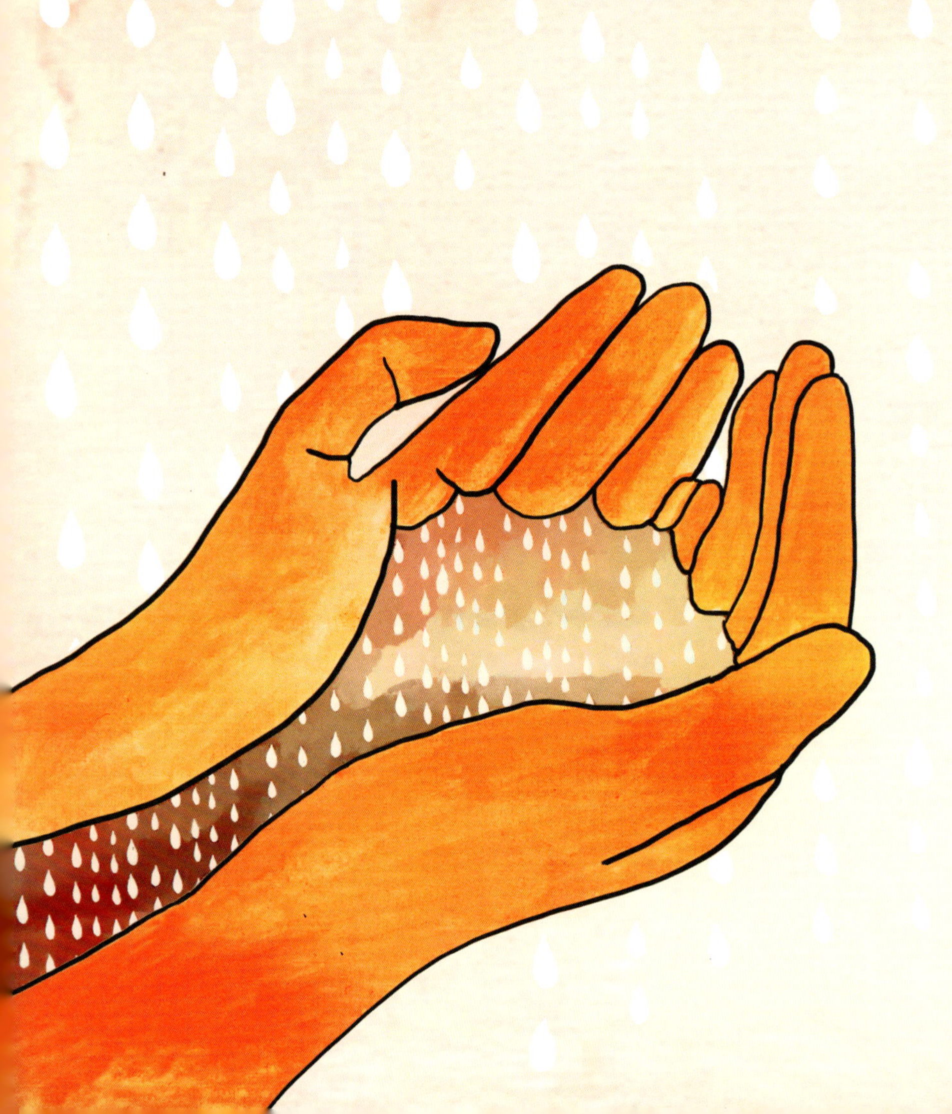

"I have always, in everything, wanted to find out things for myself."

—Amrita Sher-Gil

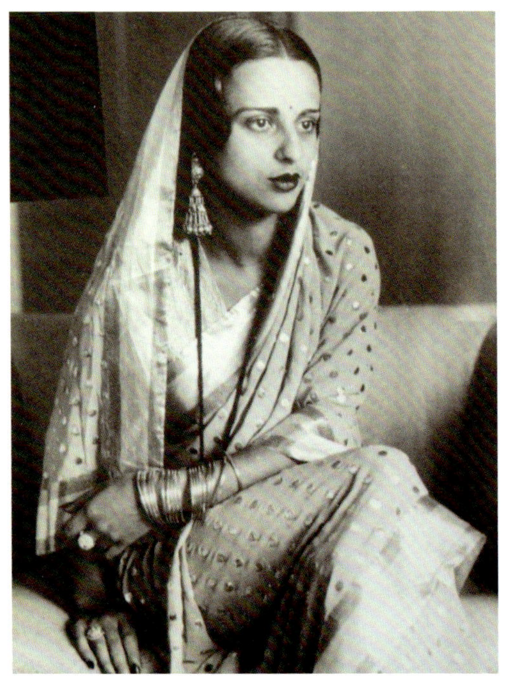

Amrita Sher-Gil, 1963. Photo likely
by Umrao Singh Sher-Gil.

# More about Amrita Sher-Gil

Amrita Sher-Gil was born on January 30, 1913, in Budapest, Hungary. Her mother, Marie Antoinette Gottesmann, was a Hungarian-Jewish opera singer. Her father, Umrao Singh Sher-Gil Majithia, was a scholar from a Sikh family in British India. Because of her mixed parentage, Amrita moved back and forth between Europe and India her entire childhood.

Amrita loved writing stories, journals, and later, letters to family and friends. But painting was what she loved most. When she was twelve, Marie took her to an art school in Italy. Amrita found the school too strict and demanded to return to India. Back in Shimla, she questioned the rituals in a Catholic convent school and was expelled. Amrita never hesitated to speak her mind.

As a teenager, Amrita's honesty and boldness were reflected in her work. She often drew nude portraits of men and women. One of her Hungarian uncles, Ervin Baktay, also an artist, encouraged Amrita to train in Paris.

Amrita was first admitted to the art institution, Grand Chaumiere, in Paris, and later to the very prestigious, École des Beaux Arts. She was mentored by Lucien Simon, a post-Impressionist artist who, in Amrita's words, "never taught art." However, he nurtured Amrita's abilities to think and express herself. Amrita also looked up to masters like Paul Cézanne and Paul Gauguin.

By the end of 1934, Amrita felt that her learning and painting in Paris were slowing down. She longed to move away from the grayness in western art and urban life. She wrote, "I began to be haunted by an intense longing to return to India, feeling in some strange way that there lay my destiny as a painter. Europe belongs

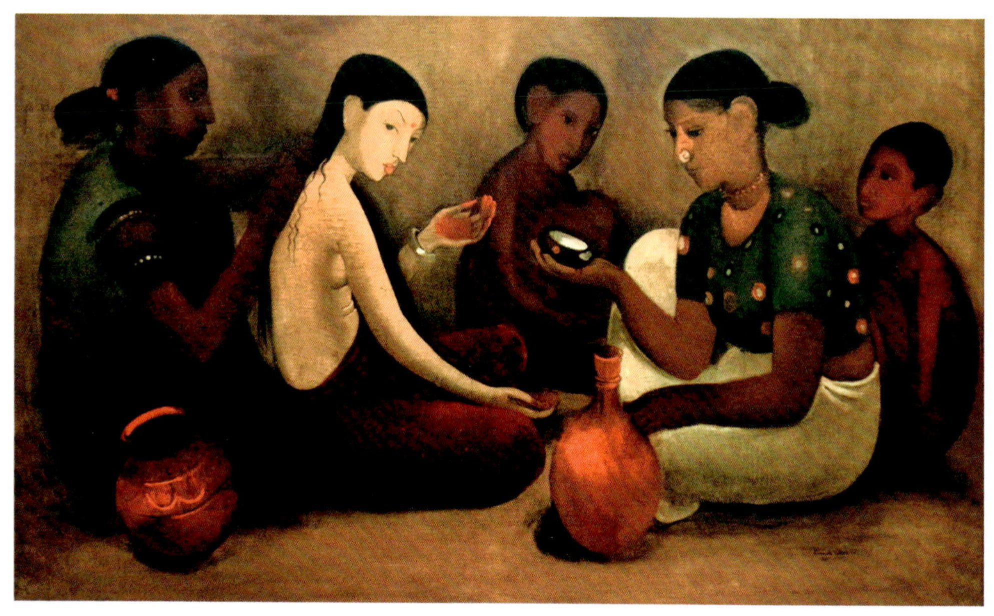

Bride's Toilet (1937) by Amrita Sher-Gil. Oil on canvas.
National Gallery of Modern Art, India.

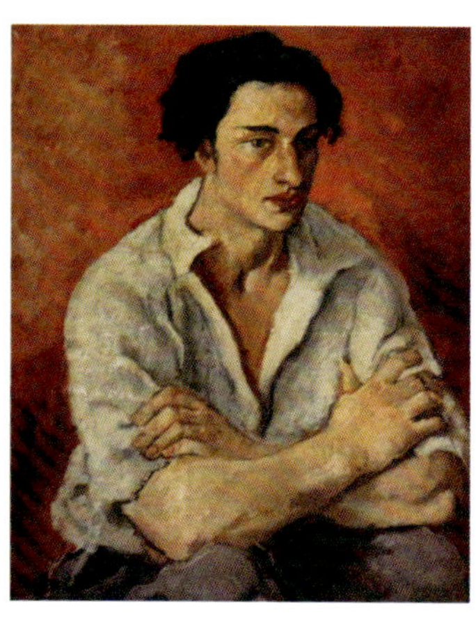

Portrait of a Young Man, Boris Tazlitsky (1930) by Amrita Sher-Gil. Oil on canvas.

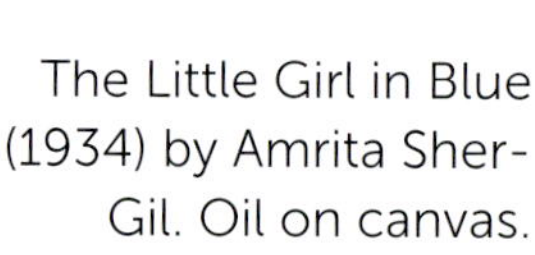

The Little Girl in Blue (1934) by Amrita Sher-Gil. Oil on canvas.

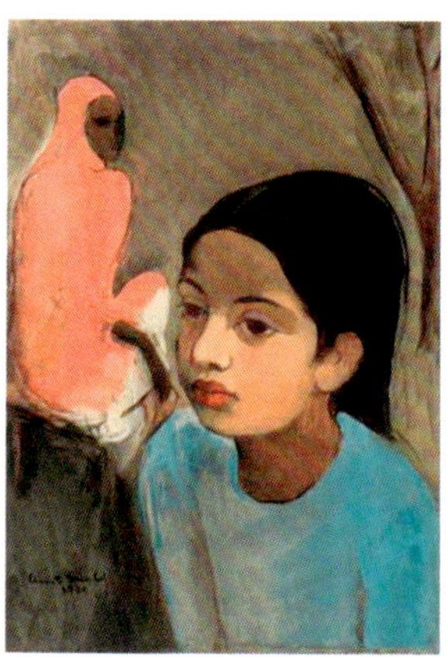

to Picasso, Matisse and Braque and many others. India belongs only to me." Amrita sailed back to India the same year. However, she eternally owed her appreciation for Indian art and sculpture to the enriching time spent in Europe.

In India, Amrita showed empathy towards poor, hardworking street and village folks. She incorporated the sadness she noticed in their eyes and body language into her paintings. At a time when Indian art mostly rested on external beauty, Amrita's work rendered genuine emotions. She questioned the norms and conventions of contemporary Indian art schools and fearlessly pursued her own aesthetics of blending western techniques with traditional Indian elements.

In 1936, Amrita went on an artistic exploration in South India where she was enthralled by the magnificence of the cave paintings in Ajanta and Ellora. Later, in the north, she was fascinated by the intricacies in (Mughal) miniature paintings. All these helped her evolve and rediscover her own voice in art.

Amrita was always close to Victor Egan, one of her Hungarian cousins; she married him in Europe in 1938. When the couple returned to India, Amrita got busy preparing for her biggest ever art exhibition in the city of Lahore. On December 5, 1941, on the eve of the big day, Amrita died, leaving behind a legacy in modern art. Today, Amrita is not only remembered for her pioneering art, but also for finding the secret to mixing her two worlds, to push boundaries and make her own space.

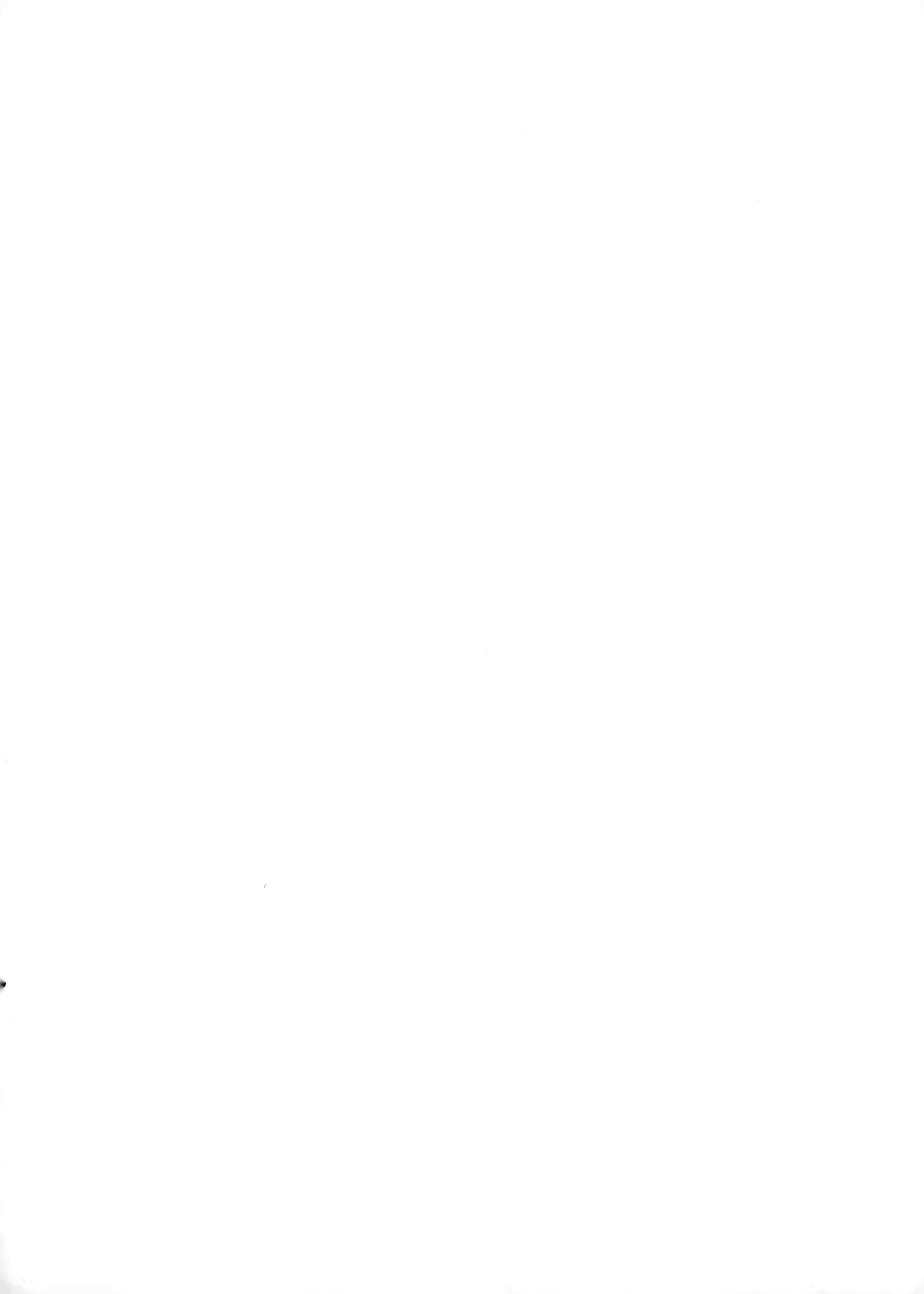

# Bibliography


Sundaram, Vivan. *Amrita Sher-Gil: A Self-portrait in Letters & Writings Volume 1.* India: Tulika Books, 2010.

Sundaram, Vivan. *Amrita Sher-Gil: A Self-Portrait in Letters & Writings Volume 2.* India: Tulika Books, 2010.

Dalmia, Yashodhara, *Amrita Sher-Gil: A Life.* India: Viking, Penguin Books India, 2006.

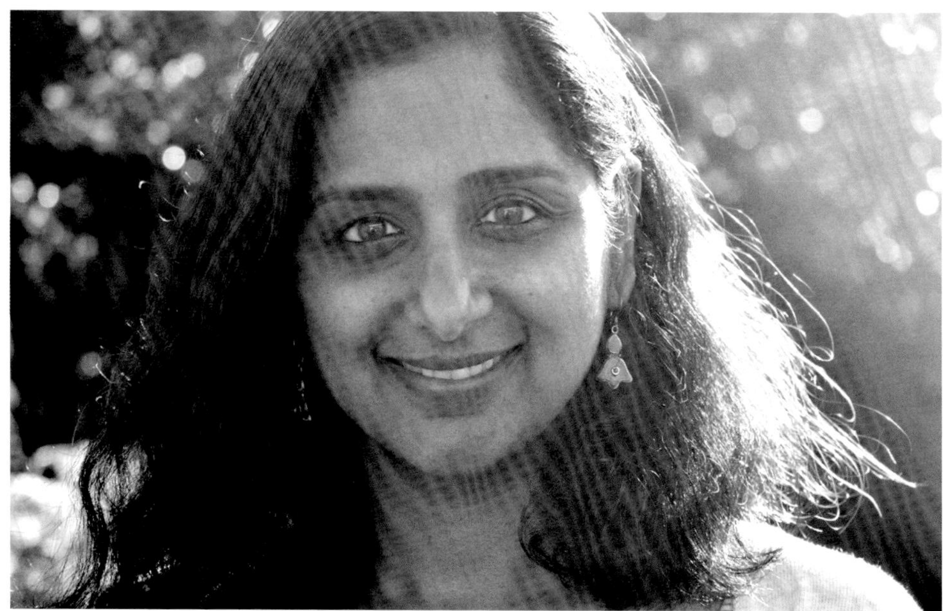

**Meera Sriram** grew up in India and moved to the US in 1999. An engineer in the past, she now enjoys writing, leading early literacy initiatives, and advocating for diverse bookshelves. Meera is the author of the picture books *The Yellow Suitcase* and *A Gift For Amma*, and has also coauthored several books in India. Meera believes in the transformative power of stories and likes to write about people, places, and experiences less visible in children's literature. For more information, visit www.meerasriram.com.

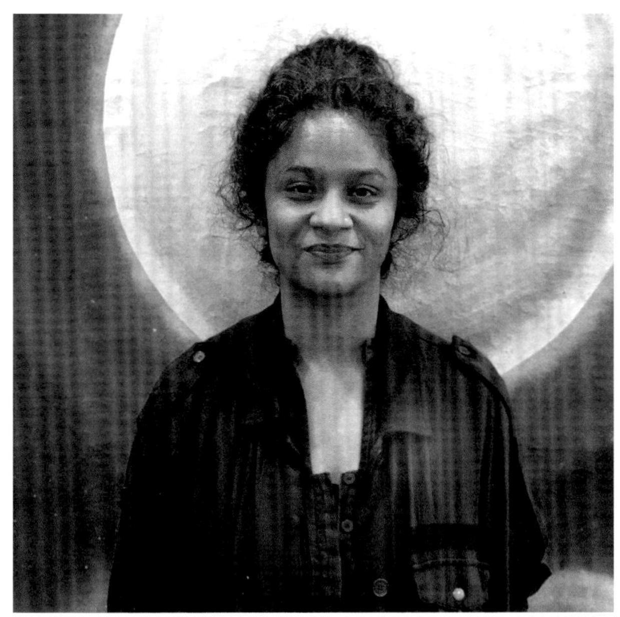

**Ruchi Bakshi Sharma** is an artist and toymaker from India. She studied Communication Design at the National Institute of Design and has several award-winning live action and stop-motion shorts to her credit. Her picaresque characters—often based on outlandish folklore—seem to inhabit a strange and wonderful world of myth and fancy. She works with multiple mediums like video art, kinetic sculptures, lenticulars, peephole boxes, paper assemblages, optical toys, animating puppets, kaleidoscopes and illustrated puzzles. Play and motion are dominant elements in her work. For more information visit https://spark.adobe.com/page/leX70jNS2Re3C/.

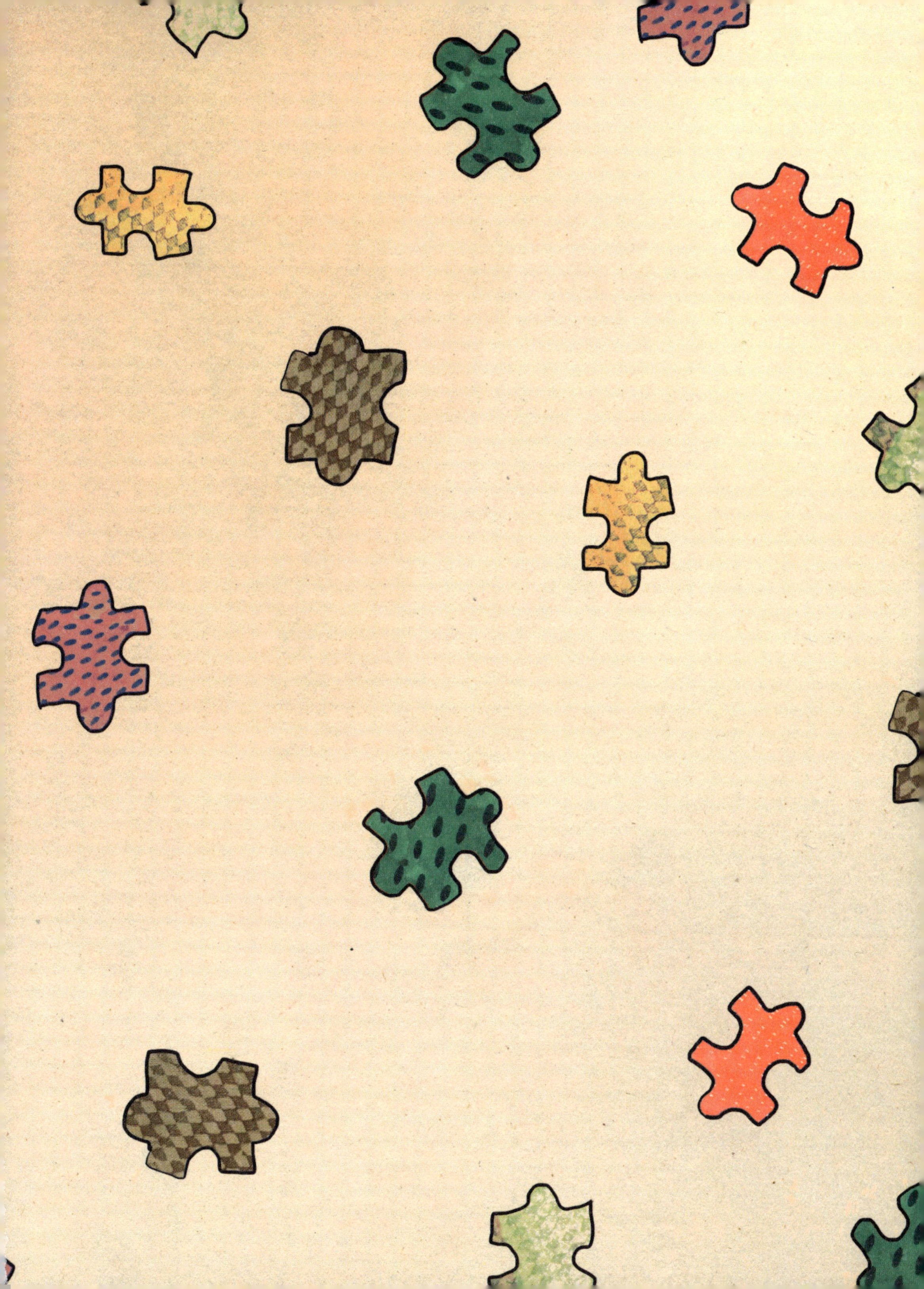

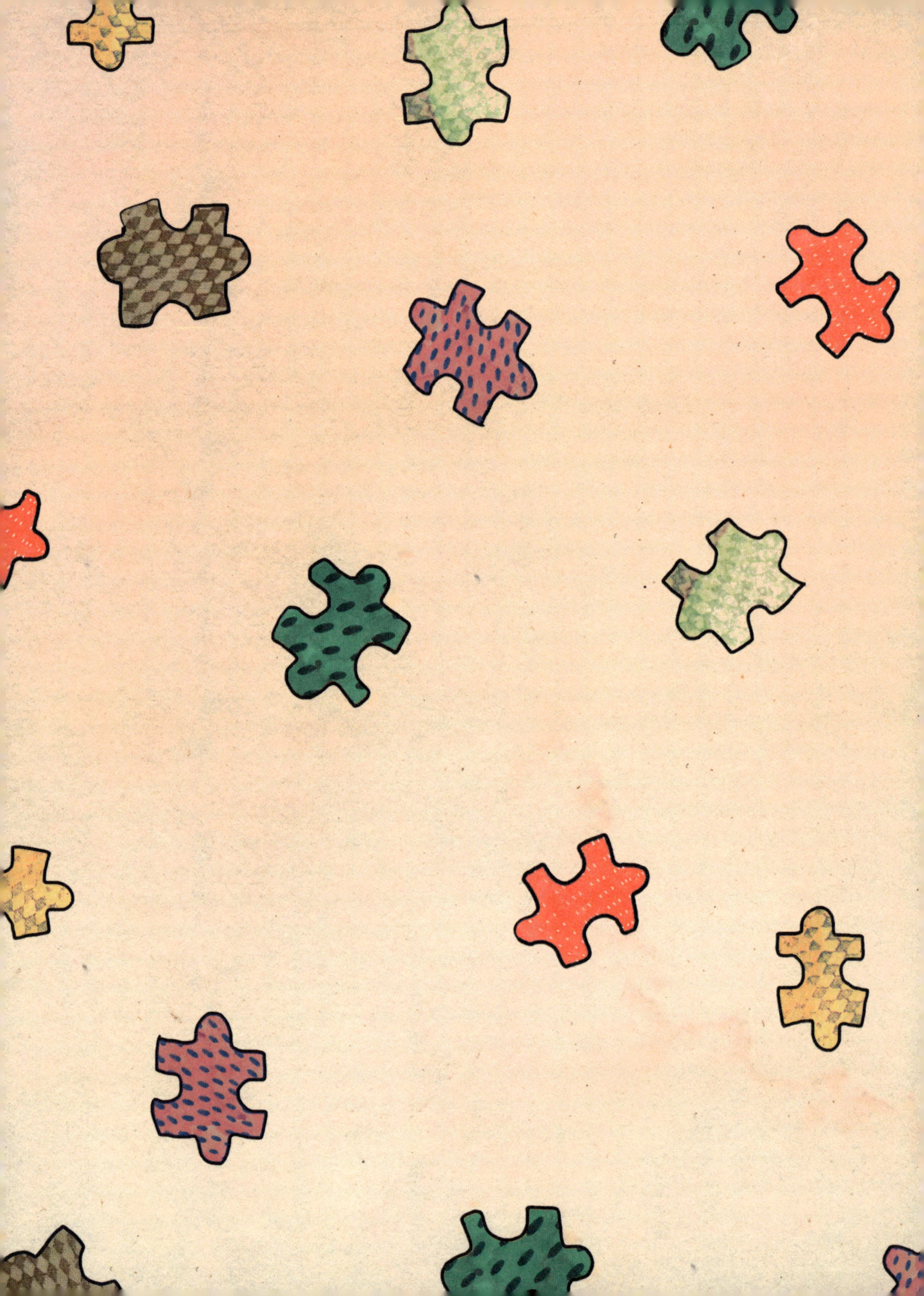